AMERICA'S
FUTURE

AMERICA'S FUTURE

Transition to the 21st Century

William H. Boyer

PRAEGER SPECIAL STUDIES • PRAEGER SCIENTIFIC

New York • Philadelphia • Eastbourne, UK
Toronto • Hong Kong • Tokyo • Sydney

Library of Congress Cataloging in Publication Data

Boyer, William H. (William Harrison), 1924–
America's future.

Bibliography: p.
Includes index.
1. Planning—United States. I. Title.
HD87.5.B68 1984   361.6'0973   83-27021
ISBN 0-03-071121-5 (alk. paper)

Published in 1984 by Praeger Publishers
CBS Educational and Professional Publishing
a Division of CBS Inc.
521 Fifth Avenue, New York, NY 10175 USA

456789 052 987654321

Printed in the United States of America
on acid-free paper

To my wife, Ann,
whose support and assistance as editor-critic
throughout the many months of research, writing, and revision
were indispensable to the completion of this book

Acknowledgments

I am grateful for the many useful suggestions made on the first draft of the manuscript by A. Daniel Burhans, George Kent, Arthur Pearl, and Sidney Peck. Shirley Suttles's editorial assistance was very valuable in helping me improve the readability of the text.

Contents

Introduction:
Designing the Future

If we are to see the dawn of the twenty-first century, we need imaginative and bold initiatives to move from current global crises toward ways of making the transition from the 1980s to the year 2,000. We have not been solving most of the problems of the human race. We have made significant achievements, especially in the control of diseases—smallpox, polio, syphilis, plague. But widespread poverty, the progressive degradation of our environmental life-support system, and the threat of thermonuclear war remain. And, we are not moving closer to any solutions. How we may see our problems clearly, identify their basic causes, agree upon values, set transitional and ultimate goals, and reach those goals by means of achievable steps are the central concerns of this book.

To accomplish all this, we must find a different way of conducting our politics and a different approach to problem solving. At this eleventh hour, we can no longer continue to hope that somehow, without our doing anything more than what we have been doing, the next year, the next decade, the next century will be better than the last. If we want a basis for such optimism, we must act to create it.

Before the age of applied science and industrialism, people led lives circumscribed by tradition and given meaning by ritual and myth. The idea of social progress and its equation with the passage of time did not enter into the way they viewed life, which they saw as fateful and inherently tragic.

During the last three hundred years, the applications of science to industry and trade produced fundamental change in people's lives, and with it, a culture optimistic about change itself. Believing that the direction of history was inexorably progressive, people began increasingly to equate time with progress. Personal know-how, ambition, and hard work would provide access to all that progress delivered, and we would all have a better life than our parents. Each generation, then, would move "upward." Trends, in this view of things, were perceived as categorically for the better.

Beginning mainly in the 1930s, statistical data about trends armed us with more precise information on change; now we could anticipate the future and profit by it. Trends for the stock market, for real estate prices, employment figures, the GNP, inflation, monetary flow, birth rates, and death rates helped people to predict change more accurately and to maximize its advantages. In this way the old faith in inherent progress was given statistical assistance.

For the past two decades, the same belief in historical forces has dominated visions of the future. Market trends have been central for capitalists, the dialectic of the class struggle central for Marxists. However, forecasters began adding a range of possibilities to projections of the future, producing some possible futures that were negative, even catastrophic. Pessimism and uncertainty increasingly replaced optimism, and the 1970s saw a major collapse of the religion of inherent progress that had sustained the modern world.

In a new, emerging view, people are in charge of social futures. Trends do not predetermine the course of history; rather, social, cultural, institutional, economic, and political aspects of human life are seen as having been invented by people; therefore, people can reinvent them. If we identify alternative futures, human values and ethics become central to our choice of the best among the alternatives. Value-centered choices of procedures and policies will replace scenario forecasting and mere adjustment to trends. The future can then be the result of intentional democratic social planning.

America's Future is based on the use of this last method of creating the future, one which has been put into practice in some limited ways, such as in new forms of land use planning, but which has not yet been applied significantly to the basic issues of war, poverty, the environment, or human rights. The time for that application is now.

Many Americans who have lost faith in inevitable progress are, however, not yet willing to accept the kind of democratic political planning which this book advocates. Frustrated and pessimistic about large-scale institutions of any type, they fear being cogs in an increasingly complicated and impersonal world. Opposed to large-scale planning, they nevertheless cannot escape the power of large-scale institutions, for we are all affected by energy costs, inflation, pollution, conscription, unemployment, taxes, and war. This group has significant impact on American politics by avoiding politics. Opting out, they hand over political power to others by default and reinforce the very institutions they most dislike.

Ironically, they are aided in achieving the same undesired objectives by a large number of other Americans who are politically active. This group views government as by nature wasteful and unproductive, and

·they believe the best government is the least government. By weakening government through the policies, the legislation, and the candidates they support, they too contribute to the very kind of wasteful and unproductive government they deplore.

As for those who want better government, they often do not achieve their objectives because of their failure to understand the basic causes of the social problems they would like to solve. Failing to understand why and how these problems have developed, they cannot identify appropriate solutions. The centers of power, such as corporations, nations, and military complexes, are then able to create the future for themselves, often without consideration for members of society for whom these institutions were ostensibly formed.

Those who want better government need first to distinguish between *precipitating* causes and *basic* causes. For example, if someone dies of a "heart attack" caused by arteriosclerosis, was the heart failure the cause of death? Or was the victim's high-fat diet and lack of exercise the main cause of the heart attack? The heart failure was the precipitating cause of death, but most deaths from heart failure could be avoided through reduced fat consumption and increased exercise. If a society emphasizes bypass surgery, it focuses on precipitating causes. If it emphasizes diet and exercise, it focuses on basic causes.

The same distinction can be applied to social problems such as war. Was the basic cause of the Argentine attack on the Falkland Islands the belief of the Argentinians that the Falklands were rightfully theirs? Or, was that the precipitating cause, the basic cause being the lack of a system of law between nations, so that no conflict mangement or peacekeeping force exists to control military violence and adjudicate disputes? With the lack of world law and institutionalization of global anarchy, military power is the ultimate authority of the international system. In this "war system" it is as normal to have wars as it is to have heart failures with high-fat diets and lack of exercise.

A precipitating cause of poverty might be high unemployment resulting from high interest rates; high prices and low wages could also be precipitating causes. But a basic cause may be that a market system of economic production and distribution is used to allocate resources, prices, wages, and job opportunities. A market system normally has booms and busts. It dispenses income unequally and insures wide economic disparity between groups. Therefore poverty, especially relative poverty, is normal under such a system.

Ecological destruction can be similarly understood. A precipitating cause may be industrial contamination of ground water through disposal of toxic waste. But when the main goal for economic production is to maximize profit for individuals and corporations and when government minimizes regulation of business, it is normal to have pollution and progressive destruction of the life-support system.

Making this distinction between precipitating and basic causes is crucial if we are to begin to solve our major problems.

Minor tinkering will not transform a firmly established system that has its own power and inertia. But the war, poverty, and ecocide (ecological destruction) systems are not like the natural systems of biology and physics. As systems of our own making, they can be dismantled and restructured by us, their inventors. We must make public decisions about the kind of society we really want, and then we must plan and implement political and economic rules and procedures that will normally produce our desired outcomes. Such action will give us, rather than the disconnected, goal-less, contradictory, band-aid efforts we ordinarily use, a cumulative sequence of changes toward a better future.

In the following chapters I shall explain in more detail how basic changes are possible in these social systems that threaten human survival. I shall also propose a strategy for integrated transition planning toward a twenty-first century with significantly greater human rights and a high quality of life. In the Appendix, I include a glossary of terms and definitions appropriate to this new future. The last chapter provides criteria for evaluating current politics and for developing public policy appropriate to the problems of this period of history.

AMERICA'S
FUTURE

1

Macrosystems:
War, Ecocide, and Poverty

War, environmental destruction (ecocide), and poverty are not accidents. They result from the way we have planned our economic and political system, and they can be largely eliminated if we plan differently.

Large-scale social systems that are national or global are macrosystems. Some are intentionally created; some are by-products of older ways of conducting politics and economics. Chattel slavery was an intentional macrosystem in early America. Once blacks could be legally bought and sold as property, the consequences were predictable. War, ecocide, and poverty are equally predictable under current political and economic rules, even though they are not explicit objectives.

The way we organize and structure politics and economics is crucial in determining our survival and the quality of our lives. If political goals guide the use of technology into the improvement of living conditions, we have planned humanely. If political goals permit runaway technology so that technology creates its own purposes, we have planned pathologically. This was true when gunpowder was developed. It is devastatingly true now that nuclear weapons have been invented.

Without adequate planning we muddle from one crisis to another and expect elected officials to fix specific problems rather than change a system that may be causing the problem. Unemployment, crime, specific wars, pollution, and even cancer are primarily by-products of political, economic, and environmental systems. Failure to identify basic structural causes of social issues prevents us from solving most of our problems. Instead they are compounded until we are deluged with daily impressions of a world out of control in which conflict, suffering, and tragedy becomes standard media fare and even a form of entertainment. We get the feeling we live in a hopeless world, and often treat politics comically or cynically and explain the perceived hopelessness as a product of human nature.

Our disconnected way of understanding the human condition and human prospects is fundamentally obsolete. It causes us to convert pessimism into a self-fulfilling prophesy, to reinforce current politics by default, and to think of ourselves as spectators of a modern version of the fall of Rome.

Understanding of our predicaments and some of the most hopeful ways of solving them is rarely apparent through news media and even through most schooling. However, hidden from the public view, a substantial body of knowledge is available which focuses on systems change and planning. This knowledge can help people control the political and economic systems on which their future depends. I will attempt to explain how war, ecocide, and poverty can be understood as a system which can and should be transformed so that we can have control over our institutions and have a basis for an optimistic future.

THE WAR SYSTEM

The *war system* under which we now live had its inception in 1648 in the Peace of Westphalia, which established the rules of the modern nation state. The nation state was to be the political entity for law and order; relations between nation states were to be controlled by trade, diplomacy, treaties, and the use of military power located within each nation.

Each nation was expected to have a military system to serve the will of the nation, but nations were obligated to respect the "sovereignty" of other nations. Since there was no enforceable international law, when conflicts arose that were not solved through diplomacy based on mutual interests, military violence was inevitably the ultimate authority.

This war system, which we have lived under ever since, constitutes a system of global anarchy in which the most powerful nations are the dominators, with violence institutionalized as the ultimate deciding force. The dominators and the nations in control have always been those with the greatest capacity to kill and destroy, that capacity being based on numbers of soldiers, amount of equipment, levels of technological advancement, quality of organization and training, and economic support and resource control to permit sustained war.

Enforceable law occurs *within* nations, where anarchy is replaced by legal processes. Military power is replaced by police, who are supposed to use minimum violence to maintain order, allowing conflict to be managed through civil courts. Without a stable system of law, there might well be internal armed groups who would then take on the characteristics of nations in the international system and thus produce civil war. This instabililty would ordinarily be resolved through a unified political system based either on autocratic or democratic power.

Conflict within and between nations is normal. It need not result in war. With a change in the rules of the world politics, conflicts can be resolved between nations in the same way they are resolved within nations, through established procedures such as elections, collective bargaining, mediation, common communication, more equitable laws, arrests, fines, etc. When violence is used by a person or an organization within a nation, that action constitutes "outlaw" action, and police action is required and expected. Murder within a nation represents the most extreme violation of human ethics. Yet when a nation sends military forces to serve the "interests" of the state (as in Vietnam), the soldier is supposed to murder as ordered or risk being murdered by his own military group, if he should disobey. Civilization has been institutionalized within nations; barbarism and anarchy have been institutionalized between nations. Peacekeeping systems have been developed within nations. But the international system is a war system.

War is a function of the rules that have been established as conventions. There is nothing about the nature of people that requires war or military systems, though myths about innate evil or aggression have been used to treat war as inevitable. Cooperative agreements have been established between nations to permit travel, economic exchange, and many forms of human cooperation, such as transmission of mail and weather information. These are, however, voluntary arrangements which can be terminated by unilateral authority of a nation.

But the price people pay for national sovereignty and war increases exponentially according to the level of technology. With nuclear explosives and ICBMs the price for war has not only increased by a quantum leap, but the war system has itself become dysfunctional. *Nuclear-armed nations no longer have national defense.* They cannot protect themselves from other nuclear nations, or from the fallout of their own weaponry. Though the words "national defense" are still used, the notion of national defense is based on the increasingly vain hope that the threat of offensive attack will deter. In World War II nations had some capacity to intercept and defend, but reality has been captured by word games such as "defense," "anti-ballistic missiles," "deterrence," and "civil defense." The word does not make reality, and defense capacity has disintegrated into mutual vulnerability. In our present age, large-scale war is mutual annihilation.

President Kennedy, even in the early sixties, saw that the deterring effect of nuclear threat would not operate under conditions of "accident, miscalculation, and madness." Unfortunately, these three factors are very much a part of the international system, especially when our highly complicated electronic systems can confuse flying geese with flying missiles. Jonathan Schell pointed out (in 1982) that:

"on three occasions in the last couple of years, American nuclear forces were placed of the early states of alert: twice because of the malfunctioning of a computer chip in the North American Air Defense Command's warning system, and once when a test tape depicting a missile attack was inadvertently inserted in the system.[1]

The normal psychology of people is to add technology to a faltering system to make it work — more ICBMs, more sophisticated surveillance, and outer-space warfare. Yet, if the social system is dangerously obsolete, the ever more fanatical attempt to make it work through technology becomes insanity.

The perpetuation of social systems that threaten the survival of people has been recorded by Arnold Toynbee in his studies of civilizations. Some civilizations responded adequately to dire challenges and survived and flourished. Some did not respond adequately and perished. In our period of history the threat is not to one of various civilizations but to all human civilization, for the effects of large-scale war can now be global. People who want us to be prepared to accept and survive World War III are asking for the most massive holocaust in human history. Moreover, if there *were* human survivors, they would soon, if the war system remained intact, create World War IV. Perpetuation of a pathological system is pathological. New learning is required to understand and transform the structure of a political system.

Designing a Twenty-first Century Peacekeeping System

The necessary peacekeeping system would require authority from a world court and would need an administrative system with jurisdiction over nations. The relationship between such an authority and nations might be roughly the same as between the federal government and state government, except that an effective peacekeeping system need not require a large centralized world government. Nations could continue to do much of what they currently do, except that they would have to limit their arms to what is needed for internal police action. In a phased disarmament, we would build the structure of the legal executive-police force so that each phased drop in military-based security would be replaced by phased-in increases in the world peacekeeping system. This new structure might be thought of as a transnational or supranational system of national defense. National security would be greatly increased, and at a fraction of the economic costs of current national military systems.

No such peacekeeping system will come into being without either the horrendous learning experience of nuclear war (if we are left to establish anything after such a learning experience) or, let us hope, public understanding of the counterproductive obsolescence of the present system. This understanding is now developing and is producing political pressures that can lead to replacement of the war system; but we must also understand that halting the current arms race is only the first step toward survival. The next step is transition planning to move from a war system to a peacekeeping system. The third step is establishing a broad base of worldwide political power to build the necessary institutions for both peacekeeping and other forms of cooperation.

Nations have difficulty proposing anything that would lessen their power, and a global peacekeeping system requires transference of some national sovereignty. Yet, the nation state is already losing its power to defend itself, and transformation of the war system has many benefits, especially economic benefits, in addition to the overpowering benefit of survival.

Widespread ignorance about the nature of war, economic involvement in the military-industrial complex, and the lack of planning experience in long-range systems change keep the old system intact. Even the use of word magic like "national defense" has enormous power in perpetuating the old system. Prior to the 1950s the military was under what was then correctly called the *War Department*. Changing the name to the *Defense Department* after World War II has greatly increased support for budgets. People are more willing to spend for "defense" than for "war."

Military spending was once widely believed to provide prosperity and jobs, but economists have ample evidence that military spending, compared to the various other ways in which the money could be spent, produces the least number of economic benefits. The economic multiplier is low, resulting in loss of employment and less stimulation to the economy than any other form of expenditure. The money goes increasingly to engineers and scientists who would be employed anyway, while the brain drain to military production weakens consumer industries and reduces national capacity for international economic competition. It also uses up resources and increases inflation by reducing the supply of the consumable gross national product and by manufacturing at inflated cost-plus prices. It shifts priorities and takes funds from social programs affecting the poor. It is, therefore, a substantial economic liability.[2]

Transition requires conversion to a peacetime economy which will shift military spending in such a way that reduction of the military budget will not threaten jobs. Such planning should provide many economic conversion incentives, but if disarmament is undertaken without economic planning for peace, it will almost certainly fail. Many people would be faced with financial threat as the funds are withdrawn from military spending without being shifted to the civilian sector in a way that gives them economic security.

A poorly managed economy uses military enlistments as a way to drain off unemployment, especially among minorities. This arrangement appears to lessen social conflict resulting from unemployment; but by letting the polictical system, business, and unions off the hook for solving unemployment and poverty, this use of military enlistment only exacerbates the root causes. Enlistees learn very few skills useful for civilian life. The are taught unquestioning obedience and are encouraged to kill under orders. Authoritarianism and weapons skills for killing lessen the capacity of young people to participate in the formation of a democratically based cooperative society. The young who avoid the military are given a head start in the civilian economy and have cumulative competitive advantages.

Transition to a peacekeeping system requires widespread public study and discussion of the systemic nature of war and its current suicidal level of development. It also requires public involvement in the design of a twenty-first century peacekeeping system and participation in the transition initiatives that must be undertaken. There is almost no chance that such a transition will occur without widespread debate, education, and dialogue on the nature of war, peace, and transition. Schools, colleges, universities, and media, therefore, have a major role in aiding public education. Virtually every organization and institution — business, unions, churches, environmental organizations, etc. — has a vital stake in war prevention and needs to confront the issues and facilitate education and political participation among its members.

To effect this transition, we need worldwide political and educational movements. By the early eighties political peace-oriented activity was under way in Western and Eastern Europe where massive rallies and protests were on the increase. The United States and Japan followed. Popular disarmament movements have been promoted in Europe by the threat posed by American nuclear bases, which many Europeans believe could turn their land into a nuclear battlefield. Many Europeans view this development as the export of holocaust away from the United States.

Along with the initiatives of the mass movements in Europe for the prevention of nuclear war, there has been an upsurge of mass peace movements in the United States. Groups such as the Physicians for Social Responsibility have countered the habit of "denial" of reality by trying to convince the American public that there is no medical treatment after atomic war and that prevention of nuclear war is the only path to survival.[3] In 1982 a grassroots movement in support of a freeze in the research, development, and deployment of nuclear weapons swept the country, to the amazement of many political officials. State elections in 1982 included many initiatives for a nuclear freeze and nearly all of them received electoral support. In May 1983 the U.S. House passed a nuclear freeze resolution by 278–149, and the U.S. Roman Catholic bishops took a stand against nuclear war by approving a pastoral letter condemning the nuclear arms race and calling for a halt to the development, production, and deployment of nuclear weapons. The statement opposed first use of nuclear weapons and stressed the unlikelihood that limited nuclear war would ever meet the church's criteria for a "just war" of legitimate self-defense.

The beliefs that have sustained the war system have begun to disintegrate. Civil defense has been rejected by many American cities as not feasible in nuclear war and, moreover, contributing to war by suggesting that nuclear war is survivable. Government proposals to wage war in outer space with exotic technology have been largely rejected by experts and by the public. Public rejection of technical solutions to war is an important element in transition, for it turns attention to political alternatives. The tradition that technology will save us and that all problems have technological solutions is deeply ingrained in American culture and will die hard. But with enough education, it will die.

Loss of faith in the institution of war can spread rapidly throughout the world if the economic costs, the erosion of real national security, and the possibility of political alternatives are made visible. The anti-war movement has been more successful in protesting current policies than in illuminating alternatives, however. It is time to bring attention to bear on long-range goals and transition steps.

At this time there is virtually nothing being publicly discussed or debated that identifies steps after the freeze. A nuclear freeze or moderate disarmament would stop the escalation of overkill, but it would not stop nuclear war unless the initial disarmament steps were tied to world law goals and a movement toward a supranational system of national security.

Movement toward a world security system would require elimination of much current unilateral and bilateral diplomacy. Regional disputes such as in Lebanon or Central America should be settled for the next few years through multilateral regional organizations involving all parties to the dispute. National governments, revolutionaries, the United States, and the Soviet Union are all needed in areas such as Lebanon and Central America. When the United States or the Soviet Union provides aid or subversion, it is playing a kind of super-power politics which fails to develop the cooperative political structures that are needed as steps in the building of new institutions.

The perceived intransigence of the Soviet Union by the United States and of the United States by the Soviet Union is partly real and partly a function of the war system which makes suspicion normal, for each side learns to be Machiavellian and to expect the worst behavior from the other side.

The built-in paranoia of national perspectives plus the fact that leaders of nations cannot be expected to take the initiatives necessary to achieve transition from the war system means that public groups must assume leadership. National leaders achieve their position by acquiring power, not by giving it up. It is romantic to expect the head of a nation to create voluntarily a limited world government which would eliminate some of the sovereignty on which his/her power rests.

Public pressures such as the global arms freeze movement are required to force political figures to make concessions or lose their political power. A representative, senator, or president who supports the arms race and is voted out of office and replaced by someone who supports transition to world law will provide a signal to other political figures of the direction the political wind is really blowing.

Transnational groups — religious, professional and business groups, labor unions, and unaffiliated individuals — need to learn to increase their political power and to offer long-range transition plans that turn the "freeze" into a first step. This process is already under way within the Catholic Church, The World Council of Churches, some organizations of attorneys, and other professional groups. Unions are beginning to perceive how a militarized economy threatens their jobs.

These nongovernmental organizations need to use their political power to achieve some direct representation in the General Assembly of the United Nations through charter revision, then later convert the United Nations to a stronger political institution which includes direct representation from the public, voted through regular elections. United Nations representation is now comparable to a hypothetical procedure whereby governors of states, elected by the public, might then select the president of the United States. A more effective United Nations needs more direct representation, more non-national fiscal support, more long-range planning, and corresponding charter revision.

With charter revision the United Nations might serve as the main peacekeeping institution while the World Court would have jurisdiction over international disputes. The economic incentives for such changes are rapidly increasing now that nations, especially the Soviet Union and the United States, are threatening their economic prosperity and standards of living with the burden of their skyhigh budgets. If poor countries received some of the savings from the demilitarization of developed countries, the political support base for achieving a revised United Nations Charter would be greatly strengthened.

THE ECOCIDE SYSTEM

Ecocide means the killing of ecological systems. The term "ecocide system" refers to the destructive effects of economic activities on the biological life support system resulting from inadequate social rules for protecting the environment. Ecocide is the by-product of obsolete economics resulting from a failure to plan economic activity within the carrying capacity of the biosphere. When economic objectives have a higher priority than preservation of the biological environment, various degrees of ecocide are inevitable.

The ecocide system is not an intentional system, but it is no less real and pervasive than if it were .intentional. The planning that causes it is usually short range and intended to serve the immediate interests of the people undertaking the economic activity. The effect of the activity on air, water and land is to lessen the capacity of the earth to support human life because ecological systems deteriorate. The environment is polluted and depleted of nutrients. Destructive change in a local ecosystem — a river, the air in a valley, or the topsoil on a few farms — may be reversed without long-term effects, but if there continues to be persistent and systematic damage to the life-support system on a worldwide basis, the social, political, and economic institutions that cause this suicidal degradation must be considered unethical and even pathological. All institutions have an impact on our environment, and they cannot be life-affirming institutions if they produce irreversible degradation of the biosphere. The life-support system is the *real* "bottom line."

Environmental degradation is commonplace throughout the world in both industrial and relatively nonindustrial countries. Environmental impacts have risen exponentially since World War II as industrial development, molecular chemistry, and high consumption, high waste, throw-away economics have flourished.

Of course, ecosystems have sometimes been deteriorated even by nature, through volcanic eruptions, for example. The Thames River of old London, and even the downwind smoke from the camp fires of ancient people can be cited as examples of preindustrial pollution. But the large-scale extraction of coal and petroleum is recent, and the magnitude of modern ecocide is becoming planetary, degrading the ozone layer of the ionosphere, carrying pollutants through all the oceans of the world, and producing enough heat from combustion and the hothouse effect in the atmosphere to warm the planet. Small increases in atmospheric temperature can melt polar ice caps, raise ocean levels, alter weather, and create deserts in place of rich farmland. Deforestation is changing weather, altering water supplies, producing deserts, and carrying topsoil from mountains into rivers and oceans, depleting nutrients for future forests and contaminating the breeding grounds of fish. Excessive extraction of water from aquafers is depleting and poisoning water supplies. Nonindustrial countries are rapidly following industrial nations in deforestation, while the plant life needed to absorb the worldwide increase in carbon dioxide and to produce oxygen is being reduced. The carbon dioxide increase comes mainly from petroleum through automobile internal combustion engines. But the overriding form of ecocide that can lie ahead is nuclear, radioactive waste from nuclear power plants and massive radioactive contamination and destruction of the protective ionosphere from nuclear war. Much of the planet, possibly all of it, could be unliveable for hundreds of years and dangerous for thousands of years. The "nuclear winter" caused by atmospheric dust from large scale nuclear war is likely to destroy plant and animal life throughout the world as drastically as when the dinosaur era was abruptly terminated.

Systems Change

Changing the ecocide system is conceptually very easy but politically very difficult. Conceptually the problems arise mainly from giving priority to economic objectives over ecological objectives. We have managed our society so that production of goods and services and economic profit have been first, and a sustainable and healthful biosphere has been a distant second. In the conflicts between the two, the life-support system has usually been degraded or destroyed to serve acquisitive economic values.

The ecocide model: Priorities
1. Economics
2. Ecology

If economic activities were constrained to include what is possible within the carrying capacity of the life-support system, there would be no ecocide.

The survival model: Priorities
1. Ecology
2. Economics

The ecocide model gives the starting point for transition. The survival model gives us the twenty-first century goal by which planned incremental transition can occur during the next 20 years.

Such transition is excessively hazardous without planning, but it does not follow that we can count on *economic* planning *per se* to avoid ecocide. Whether it be the communist planning of the Soviet Union and China, the socialist planning of Yugoslavia, or the mixed planning of Northern Europe, the goals of *economic* growth have usually been paramount. The Soviet Union and China have been great planners: The Soviet Union depletes nonrenewable resources and produces air and water pollution, and China has considerable air pollution in its industrial cities. Much of their planning is pre-ecological and obsolete, and China is heading rapidly toward the development of environmentally dangerous industries.

Socialist and communist planning systems can constrain economic activities more easily than can market capitalism, but if the market system can be required to operate within the carrying capacity of the biological life-support system, it would not be incompatible with a healthy environment. Socialist economics needs similar disciplining to prevent growth and expansion of the economy from being the overriding objective. Both capitalist and socialist theory have been largely pre-ecological. Socialist priorities were concerned mainly with economic justice and capitalist priorities with production for profit, both using technology to exploit nature. Natural resources in these early models were considered, for all practical purposes, to be unlimited. Limits to growth based on scarcity was a lesson of the 1970s.

The case for ecological planning was *avant-garde* in the 1960s, but it is now commonplace in academic literature. The areas of substantial new development which can permit both economic development *and* a sustainable liveable environment include:

1. Transference from fossil fuels to solar-based energy, which is incoming and renewable. Requires goods reduction.

2. Shifts from *consumption* to *use* of nonrenewable materials so that with recycling and preservation each generation is assured access to nature's capital.

3. Control of noise and chemical pollutants through technology with enforced human rights to a clean and healthful environment.

Nuclear fission is ecologically obsolete, since it uses scarce nonrenewable resources for fuel and produces waste that is highly toxic and has long-term persistance—hundreds of thousands of years. Once in the atmosphere or in water it is irreversibly in the food chain and the environment.

Nuclear fusion, although an uncertain technology, is one that could change the future. It produces some contaminants but is much cleaner than fission, and its fuel is abundant. If the many technical obstacles are surmounted, the twenty-first century could see the use of fusion power. Even that would have limits, however, for, unlike solar-based power, it unbalances the heat of the earth by adding atmospheric heat and raising global atmospheric temperatures. Thermal pollution, with its likely drastic changes in world weather, ocean levels, and rainfall, could be the ultimate form of ecocide. Fusion is one of those unproven technologies that might be a twenty-first century bonus. Yet to assume that fusion technology will assuredly save us and to squander fossil fuels without working on rapid conversion to solar power would be a *drastic high-risk* choice. If the economics and technology of fusion did not work out, human civilization could collapse into malnutrition, disease, and poverty as the world economy rapidly ran out of fossil fuel reserves.

Running out of coal, which is a fossil fuel, would take longer than running out of petroleum, for coal is more abundant than petroleum, but the high pollutant cost of coal is a major problem, causing "acid rain" and health hazards to workers. Coal, however, offers useful transition opportunities while a sustainable thermodynamic economy in ecological balance is being created. Such an economy will be based on the many ways of capturing solar energy, including direct heat, plant photosynthesis, photo-voltaic power, ocean thermal energy conversion, hydroelectric power, and tidal power. The other side of this solar energy plan is high conservation and reduced consumption of high energy-resource based goods. But the key to the future is using less energy while also achieving a high quality of life.

Ethics and Ecocide

Pollution transfers one of the costs of production to someone else, usually someone who does not reap the economic benefits. It is, therefore, a form of exploitation. It certainly violates the creed of free enterprise, that those who get the profits should pay the costs of production. It is established ethics that we do not throw our garbage on our neighbor's lawn, yet industries put their garbage in air, water, and land that does not belong to them.

Pollution, therefore, exploits people for the profit of others, and it violates the established right to life and the emerging right to a clean and healthful environment. Environmental rights have begun to develop in statutory law, and two state constitutions, those of Michigan and Hawaii, include rights to a "clean and healthful environment."

Resource depletion, especially the consumption of nonrenewable resources, violates the rights of future generations. It provides veto power over the future use of our *common* heritage. The unborn, who lack the political power to object, have their rights stolen. As yet there is little legal protection for the environmental rights of future generations.

When profit making on the part of individuals and corporations is the unconstrained rule of the economic game, the short-range, *ad hoc*, self-interest, competitive aspects of social behavior will make it unlikely that either a larger public interest or the interests of future generations will be served. Lack of adequate constraints over such a system can even produce large-scale death through pollution and starvation if the life-support system and its resources continue to be mismanaged. The loss of minerals, topsoil, and fossil fuels also has high impact on quality of life.

Systems change requires that the life-support system, which includes nonrenewable resources, be given greater political protection. Current planning practices often include public hearings of all interested parties, ostensibly to treat all interests as equal, presupposing equality of claims. In practice, costs and benefits are often analyzed but measured only in terms of *economic* costs and benefits. The economic standards override ethical claims.

Twenty-first century goals need to include environmental rights comparable to the priority concern for civil liberties which are constitutionally guaranteed in the Bill of Rights. Such rights are not measured in terms of predominant votes at a public meeting or in terms of economic costs or benefits. Constitutional rights are *a priori*. Claims based on *personal* wants, desires, and preferences are secondary claims to constitutional rights.

The original American Constitution did not even include a Bill of Rights. It was fought for and won by the political action of workers and farmers. Previous experience with governmental tyranny had illuminated the need to add explicit constitutional rights to protect such vital concerns as free speech and the practice of religion. We need now to incorporate the environmental considerations which bear on "the right to life" the way we once stressed "liberty" and the "pursuit of happiness" in the Declaration of Independence. But "liberty" and "happiness" now require environmental health. The "liberty" to live with noise and amidst smells of pollutants, the "happiness" that results from cancer that is environmentally caused, or the "freedom" to starve because of depleted or urbanized farmlands are hardly contributions to human progress.

To live in harmony with the biosphere presupposes applying ethical environmental principles to law and political planning. Our life and that of future generations requires changes nationally and globally in the way we treat the environment. A healthy ecosystem is essential to the quality of life and our common survival.

THE POVERTY SYSTEM

Poverty is also largely systemic. We can best attack it not with large-scale philanthropy but by discovering and changing the rules that create and support it.

Poverty can be defined either broadly as a low quality of life or, in economic terms, as lack of goods and services. Changing quality-of-life poverty is more difficult than changing economic poverty because cultural values, personal values, and many economic and environmental factors bear on quality of life. If poverty is defined in economic terms, as it usually is, poverty can be altered through political power by changing economic rules. Though quality-of-life poverty is the ultimate poverty, economic poverty is one major part of it.

Absolute poverty consists of economic levels so low that the very life of the impoverished is threatened by lack of such basic needs as food, clothing, and shelter. Relative poverty consists of being cut off from most or all of the goods and services members of one's society consider to be of importance. People living in relative poverty usually feel separated from most of the members of their society and are ridden with a sense of failure.

Clearly, absolute poverty is the most intolerable condition because in absolute poverty people are denied the right to life. But in relative poverty, people who are cut off from the activities and symbols that indicate success within their society are denied the right to dignity and self-respect.

Nearly all absolute poverty in the world is in nonindustrial countries often called "undeveloped" or "newly developing." Most people living in absolute poverty live in cities, many under conditions some anthropologists consider to be worse than those experienced by prehistoric people who lived by hunting and gathering.

Relative poverty exists in all countries, although the degree and severity varies greatly according to the pattern of economic distribution within each country.

Basis for Productivity

The productivity of an economy governs the amount of goods and services available for distribution and is based on factors such as the natural resources available, skills of the population, levels of technological development, economic and political organization, and human effort.

Some factors can make up for others. Japan has good farm resources but no oil and few minerals; yet, skills, technology, human effort, and organization compensate. In Israel, where there are also poor farm resources, skills, education, technology, social organization, gifts from abroad, and a highly determined effort serve to compensate. Both countries must bring in many outside natural resources, including oil, and process them for export to obtain exchange credit.

The United States, however, has been a nation of exceptionally high resource levels including farmland, lumber, oil, coal, hydro power, and water. With moderate skills, fairly high technology, moderately good organization, and average human effort, the United States produced the greatest abundance the world has ever seen until the 1970s, when per capita income in Sweden and Switzerland exceeded that of the United States. The United States is now surpassed in per capita income by a number of industrial nations, moving from first in the early 1950s to eleventh in 1982.

Even with a high GNP, the United States has always had high levels of relative poverty. During the 1970s there was a one-to-fifteen ratio in income between the top and bottom 10 percent. Only France, among the developed nations, tolerated a higher level of relative poverty, a one-to-seventeen ratio.[4] Sweden in turn has had a one-to-seven ratio. The rich did better in the United States and France, while white-collar and blue-collar workers did better in Sweden. The results were not at all accidental. They resulted from distribution rules controlled through the political system. During the Reagan administration, maldistribution has increased.

Maldistribution Factors

There is no natural distribution ratio. All distribution ratios are the result of policies and rules based on intentional design or tradition. The following conditions produce maldistribution and, therefore, relative poverty:

1. Taxes which provide consistent and cumulative advantage to some groups over others, such as capital gains exemptions which tax unearned income from capital appreciation at a much lower level than income through labor.

2. Upzoning of land to produce unearned income for more wealthy landowners, shifting inflation costs to nonlandowners.

3. Unequal bargaining power among workers, either because of lack of unionization or because of discrimination on account of race, sex, ethnic origin, or social class.

4. Low welfare levels which keep the "safety net" so low that it guarantees poverty.

5. Low inheritance taxes which provide unequal political and economic advantages for successive generations of families.

6. Few public services such as education, medicine, and transportation.

7. A graduated income tax schedule which is ineffective because of compensating loopholes.

8. Keeping scarce and nonrenewable resources in the private sector. Such resources, including land, will inflate faster than general inflation and produce unearned income among a few who are already the most wealthy.

9. Discrimination by social class for high-income jobs, through in-group selection to higher education and licensing. Law and medicine have often had such a role. In-group discrimination is commonplace for high managerial jobs.

10. Lack of employment rights, which permits government to create unemployment in the course of implementing inflation reduction.

11. Military recruitment which skims the "bottom" and keeps income levels and competitive skills low for income groups that are already disadvantaged.

12. Lack of a guaranteed income for the needy and for those who can work but have not been able to find jobs.

13. Lack of an equitable economic distribution ratio to guide public policy. Without public policy mandating greater income equality, *ad hoc* politics determine distribution fluctuations.

14. Lack of wealth and income maximums for upper limits, which are necessary if there are to be lower limits.

To achieve more equitable distribution, each of the above policies should be revised so that the economically weak are given advantages instead of the economically strong, until an ethically acceptable distribution ratio is achieved.

The Use of Myths

Pervasive myths are also important for perpetuating poverty. Here are two of the most common:

1. Those who are poor have character defects such as laziness or lack of incentive.

2. Those who are poor have genetic intellectual defects which "naturally" put them on the bottom.

These myths, known as "blame the victim," transfer responsibility for poverty to the poor on the presumption that they are inherently inferior. Therefore, society is improved by keeping the poor at the bottom since they got there through natural selection. There is no presumed need for social responsibility. Some other myths about poverty are as follows:

3. People deserve what they earn. Those with high income deserve more because they are making a proportionally higher contribution.

4. A market economy is the only economy compatible with democracy and freedom, and the inequality of distribution is a necessary price to pay for "freedom."

5. The discipline of economic threat is necessary to make people work and produce.

6. The profit motive produces creativity and leadership upon which economic progress depends.

Though all six of these beliefs are contradicted by contemporary social knowledge, they serve the purposes of ideologies that shift responsibility away from public policy. Older conceptions of individualism, religious views of sin — sloth, laziness, lack of initiative — undergird the blame-the-victim pattern. The work ethic ideology of American pioneers included such beliefs. These myths are among the most valuable capital for those who experience special advantages. Thus, there is much at stake for privileged groups in having the poor, the middle class, and the wealthy share these beliefs.

When the market is used as the explanation for an economic determinism that justifies relative poverty, the same self-serving metaphysics operates. "Laws" of supply and demand, considered part of nature, are then cited to explain low wages and unemployment. Instead of designing changes needed to reduce poverty, an extreme deterministic-market ideology presumes that we should forecast and predict what the market has in store for us so we can adapt to the inexorable trend. The "unseen hand" of the marketplace is presumed to be outside of politics in the same way that God is outside of nature. In the name of personal responsibility, these myths help eliminate collective *social* responsibility.

Solving Poverty Through Growth

One of the main reasons relative poverty has not been given much attention in the United States is that growth and expansion of the GNP has provided a basis for improvement in general living standards, even though improvements for the poor have been less than for the rich. The idea was that everyone was to be better off and that those at the low end should not be concerned with those at the upper end. "Trickle down" and the "tide that lifts all boats" were presumed to be sufficient.

The factor that was largely ignored was that big incomes for some require small incomes for others. Instead of concentrating on who gets the big slice of the pie and who gets the little slice (and who gets no pie at all), growth strategy has given almost exclusive attention to expanding the size of the pie under the label Gross National Product.

During the 1970s we made a shift to slow growth. The stimulus of the Vietnam War was over, the price of petroleum greatly increased, and the costs of the Vietnam War were being paid. White-collar bureaucratic inefficiency in government and the private sector increased, high military expenditure continued, unemployment was tolerated, labor productivity was nearing its limit, and resource scarcity was producing lower growth levels and even negative growth; the pie stopped getting larger.

But most important, we overproduced. We produced in most areas, except housing, more than people could consume. Then we stretched credit to try to get people to buy it all.

Goods production, the glutted area, relied on low-cost energy and resources to produce growth. As we move toward a service economy with a sustainable energy base, economic growth will continue to slow. Therefore, economic growth can no longer be the central strategy for alleviating poverty. The economy will become more of a zero-sum game. Each group that does not have its fair share will increasingly observe that other groups have more than their fair share.[5] The discovery of distribution planning can lead either to new political goals for economic justice or, if a just policy of income distribution between groups is ignored, to high levels of conflict and violence.

A margin of economic growth still available is in labor productivity, where the Japanese have excelled. In democratizing the means of production, output rises, employee satisfaction is also increased, and quality often rises. But the Japanese model focuses only on the *means* of production, not on its *goals*.

A human-centered economy appropriate to the twenty-first century should *increase growth in relation to human needs*. It should transfer monotonous work to technology and robots, while people who are served by the economy should have control over production and distribution.

Recent "growth" has been often toward *wants* rather than *needs* and has produced many low-quality goods and services. A sustainable survival-oriented economy would not produce as many goods but would produce better goods and more services. The resulting "pie" might not be larger but it would be much more nourishing.

Solving Poverty Through Distribution

The more equally the economic pie is distributed, the less relative poverty there will be. If the pie is large and the population is not, as in Sweden, there can be a wealthy egalitarian society.

If the pie is not large and population is large, as in China, there can be a highly equal distribution with small per capita income. India has about the same per capita income as China, but extremes in distribution have produced much more absolute poverty and death in India than in China, where greater sharing is built into political rules of distribution.

Countries such as the United States have avoided facing up to the ethical question of distribution politics by keeping alive the belief in growth and abundance. "Supply side economics," popular under the Reagan administration, focuses on increasing the amount of the GNP rather than increasing the distribution.

Both growth and distribution can be used to reduce poverty but military spending and unemployment, particularly characteristic of the Reagan administration, both produce growth reduction. Stagnant growth and depression make distribution policy even more urgent. Moving from resource and petroleum abundance to more scarce and expensive resource and energy sources adds to the urgency of distribution policy.

Integrated planning, which is directed toward sustainable forms of solar energy and combines economic justice and high common quality of life in the planning goals, would no longer ignore structural maldistribution. Instead of observing trends and commenting on them, people need to make distribution ratios an issue at every level of politics.

Basic Alternatives to Poverty

Earlier in this chapter basic macro alternatives to ecocide were shown to require a shift in macro priorities. Instead of economics being first priority and ecological considerations second, survival demands the reversal of these priorities.

Essentially the same shift is required to transform the poverty system. Whereas economic considerations have been first and social justice considerations second, it is necessary to create politics which shift marco priorities so that social justice has a higher priority than gross economic considerations.

Social justice requires the use of both poverty distinctions — absolute and relative. Clearly, the elimination of absolute poverty, which actually kills people, is the most urgent goal of social justice, especially in international planning. Although relative poverty does not kill, it has considerable effect on social conflict, the quality of life, and on personal dignity.

The war issue, the ecocide issue, and the poverty issue are tied to fundamental human rights considerations. All three bear on the right to life. Failure to support policies that can reduce death may be a form of genocide. Increasingly, it is important to apply criminal indictment when it is clear that political decision makers engage in pro-death decisions, analogous to the concept of "crimes against humanity" that arose in Nuremburg.

Currently, public failure to understand how life and death decisions are controlled by political power is an important factor in the failure to assign responsibility. Twenty-first century politics and planning will need to operate at a higher level of public understanding about social systems. Social systems education through schools and media will be a major requirement of the transition between the present and the twenty-first century.

The following illustration shows how it is possible to provide distinctions in social systems and values for an ethics-based twenty-first century political philosophy.

Systems Priorities

From (now)	To (21st century)
1. Economics	1. Environment
2. Social needs	2. Social needs
3. Environment	3. Economics

Value Priorities

1. Individual wealth	1. Human survival
2. Corporate power	2. Social justice
3. National sovereignty	3. Common quality of life

This approach makes transition the means to goals (ends), whereas we now rely largely on piecemeal muddling through, without long-range goals. If we do not have explicit social goals, the odds for averting major tragedies and having a better future will not be very high.

The odds are even lower if we concentrate on symptoms rather than causes and fail to see how parts are connected to larger systems. Short-term, piecemeal muddling is far more likely to be part of the problem than part of the solution, especially for a complex, modern society where lead time can be great, expenditures enormous, and where some errors are irreversible.

NOTES

1. Johnathan Schell, *The Fate of the Earth* (New York; Avon Books, 1982), pp. 26–27. See also Johnathan Schell, "Nuclear Arms — Part I" (*New Yorker*, Jan. 2, 1984), pp. 36–75; and "Nuclear Arms — Part II" (*New Yorker*, Jan. 9, 1984), pp. 43–94.

2. For more detailed information, see Chapter 4 on Economics.

3. See Helen Caldicott, *Nuclear Madness* (New York: Bantam, 1982).

4. See Lester Thurow, *Newsweek*, Feb. 14, 1977. Also, Lester Thurow, *Zero Sum Game* (New York: Basic Books, 1982), pp. 155–90.

5. Ibid., pp. 11–15.

SELECTED READINGS

Boyer, William. 1975. *Alternative Futures: Designing Social Change.* Dubuque, Iowa: Kendall-Hunt.

Center for the Study of Democratic Institutions, *A Constitution for the World.* 1965. Santa Barbara, California: Center for the Study of Democratic Institutions.

Clark, Grenville, and Louis B. Sohn. 1966. *World Peace Through World Law.* Cambridge, Mass.: Harvard University Press. Also, *The Introduction to World Peace Through World Law* (1967).

Falk, Richard. 1971. *This Endangered Planet.* New York: Random House.

Lifton, Robert, and Richard Falk. 1982. *Indefensible Weapons.* New York: Basic Books.

Johansen, Robert C. 1978. *Toward A Dependable Peace: A Proposal For An Appropriate Security System.* New York: Institute for World Order.

Larson, Arthur. 1964. *Questions and Answers on the World Court.* Durham, North Carolina: World Rule of Law Center, Duke University Law School.

Millis, Walter, and James Real. 1963. *The Abolition of War.* New York: MacMillan.

Rappoport, Anatol. 1974. *Conflict in Man-Made Environment*. Baltimore, Maryland: Penguin Books.

Tinbergen, Jan. Coordinator. 1976. *Reshaping the International Order*. New York: Dutton.

Watt, Kenneth, et al. 1977. *The Unsteady State*. Honolulu, Hawaii: East-West Center Press.

Woito, Robert. 1982. *To End War*. New York: Pilgrim Press.

2

Human Rights

We seem to be using the words "human rights" with increasing frequency, but what we mean by them is often vague. Do people *have* innate human rights? Or is it, rather, that for ethical reasons they *ought to have* human rights? Are civil liberties and human rights the same? What are the specific entitlements that deserve to be called rights? Moreover, with cultures and nations differing so widely, do the human rights of their members differ accordingly? Do cultures define the rights that people ought to have? Do human rights change as national borders are traversed?

Let us begin—as I think we must—with an assumption that is revolutionary in its implications: If we are talking about human rights, *human* is a definitive, operative word, and whatever rights are identified apply to all people. Subcategories, whether national, cultural, racial, or sexual, do not matter.

If one is human, one has human rights.

HISTORY

The "human rights" idea developed only in the last four centuries.[1] Ancient tribes had certain rights for their own tribal members but not for members of alien tribes. In Greece the Athenian citizen had the "right" to own slaves, but the slaves had no rights, for they were property rather than citizens. The economy of the United States was built substantially on the labor of blacks kidnapped from Africa who had no rights long after the Bill of Rights of the Constitution was developed. The Bill of Rights was for American "citizens." Blacks were the property of citizens.

Medieval kings had "divine rights" which other people did not have. The word of a king was law even over the life and death of subjects. Aristocratic societies typically did not believe that lower castes were actually members of the same "race." Rights were reserved for members of the artistocracy, the *real* persons.

Human rights were given their main intellectual credentials in the eighteenth century, at the time of the French and American revolutions, largely by intellectual humanists rather than by theologians or clerics. Documents such as the Declaration of Independence and the French Declaration of the Rights of Man were beacons ignited by a new ethic of universal humanism. Universalist religions of the East and the West supported these ideas in some measure, but they received their first legal meaning in the West. Since then, these principles, based on the presumption of inherent human rights, have been gaining legitimacy throughout the world, increasing the acceptance of the idea of a *human* race in which individual members have all rights as *members* of the human race. As this concept spread, despotism, which was legitimized throughout most of human history, has been correspondingly delegitimized.

Since World War II the principles of the American Bill of Rights and the Declaration of Independence have been repeatedly used by national movements trying to overthrow despotic Western colonial powers such as the English in India, and the French and later the Americans in Vietnam. Repressive actions of Western colonialism were often, to the chagrin of colonial powers, opposed through statements of rights that had found their inception within the colonial nations themselves. Such ideas were powerful forces in undermining support of colonialism by citizens of the colonial nations. This was one of the factors in the withdrawal of the United States from Vietnam.

Rights in the last four centuries have been not merely ideas but beliefs, often held with passion, that have provided a basis for social change, revolution, political ideology, and law. Earlier rights were pro-freedom and anti-tyranny rights based on reaction to the tyrannies of governments that had forcibly controlled the free speech of churches, the press, and the schools. Censorship is a major technique of tyranny, and so freedom of speech through the press, academic freedom, and in churches became the core of the new rights.

These rights also included rights to due process, which has meant that steps written into law to protect the innocent will not be arbitrarily bypassed by government. Constitutionally based rights helped control arbitrary executive and legislative power. We have seen these rights tested in the McCarthy period and during the presidency of Richard Nixon, and in a narrow contest, the Constitution prevailed.

NEW HUMAN RIGHTS

Civil liberties promulgated under the amendments of the Constitution still constitute one form of human rights. Civil liberties are mainly anti-tyranny rights, freedom *from* rather than freedom *to*, and in that sense are negative. In 1941 Franklin Roosevelt introduced what he called the Four Freedoms, which included not only freedom of speech and worship but also freedom from want and from fear. Freedom from fear referred mainly to national security. The third freedom, freedom from want, was soon developed into the idea of an economic bill of rights, a fundamentally new dimension. The idea of social and economic rights was moving human rights theory in the direction of positive entitlements that have increasingly been added to human rights through the statutory law of nations.

The UN Charter in 1945 pledged the member nations to cooperate in supporting human rights and produced unprecedented new levels of international support for universal rights. Within three years the UN General Assembly adopted the Universal Declaration of Human Rights, which included civil and political rights, and economic, social, and cultural rights as well. Rights were not only freedoms from governmental tyranny but *entitlements to fulfillment of basic human needs.*[2]

The post-World War II period gave rise to principles that are candidates for world law. The concept of "crimes against humanity" used in the Nuremberg trials conveyed belief in emerging supranational law by adding human responsibilities to international law, whether or not these responsibilities were part of national law. Progress in incorporating human rights into an enforceable legal system might have developed at that time, but unfortunately the Soviet-American cold war deflected and delayed this progress toward universal human rights. Human rights and the Nuremberg principles were ignored by the U.S. Government in Vietnam and were not given attention until the detente of the 1970s. The Carter administration became the first to put significant emphasis on human rights, especially with the initiative of Andrew Young, Carter's representative to the United Nations. Though Carter's foreign policy emphasized human rights limited to traditional civil liberties, the practices of foreign governments were often judged by their support or violation of such rights. South African *apartheid*, torture in Chile and South Korea, and persecution of Russian dissidents were officially condemned by the American government under President Carter. But the verbal condemnation was not followed by any policy, and increasingly the Carter administration played down human rights except when they were violated by the USSR.

The Reagan administration shifted back to a foreign policy based on national strategic interests and corporate economic interests, and matters of human rights were abandoned to private organizations such as Amnesty International and the ecumenical churches. Amnesty International has had some success in gaining release of political prisoners by harassing governments. It documents and publicizes torture, political imprisonment, and crimes committed by governments. This action has assisted other governments and world opinion in applying pressure against actions of repressive governments. No leadership for human rights has emerged from President Reagan's administration.

Human Rights and National Sovereignty

Moral authority has various dimensions. It can be cultural and local, or it can transcend nations and ethnic groups when a large number of people throughout the world believe that certain social principles are decent, right, and proper for all. Human rights have slowly achieved this universal character, particularly the right of life, freedom from torture, the right to education, freedom of speech, the right to have a job, and the right to vote. Churches, newspapers, and governments can bring pressure to bear against violations of human rights with some effectiveness when there is a wide moral consensus.

But the rising moral consensus is informal, and beyond it there is no political or legal structure which represents the human race. Therefore, when there is conflict between the heads of nations and principles of human rights, national interests come first and human rights second. This is inherent in the structure of the world political system as it is now organized.

The United States will not support human rights in another country if to do so is believed to jeopardize vital military or economic interests. The United States can give high priority or even first priority to American rights, but since the U.S. Government does not represent a world constituency, national interests will supersede human rights. This is what happened in the Carter administration, in which human rights were at first given high priority until they later were in conflict with other national interests.

The United Nations is sometimes believed to be the appropriate structure for guaranteeing human rights. However, although international coalitions and majority votes of national representatives in the United Nations may support some human rights and may verbally condemn violators, neither the United Nations nor the World Court has supranational enforcement power. The United Nations is an *international* organization representing *nations*. It has no power other than to persuade, and this means that human rights will never be enforceable without the creation of a structure that goes beyond the present UN organization and carries the authority to enforce human rights even when national governments violate them.

Clarifying the Meaning of Human Rights

What ought to be the definition of human rights? The four rights categories connected with the French and American revolutions included the right to *life, liberty,* the *pursuit of happiness* and the *ownership of property.* "Life" refers to personal survival, "liberty" is largely protection from the tyranny of the state, and "pursuit of happiness," though vague, presumably means individual opportunity to give meaning to one's life. The right to "property ownership" includes the right to own land, improvements, and commodities.

Cyrus Vance, former Secretary of State under Carter, has suggested the following way of defining rights, which extends beyond traditional definitions:[3]

1. Freedom from government violation of the integrity of the person.
2. The right to civil and political liberties.
3. The right to vital needs such as food, shelter, health care, and education.

People living in absolute poverty would give first priority to (3) "food, shelter, health care, and education," while the affluent would probably give first priority to (2) "civil and political liberties." Freedom from (1) "government violation of the integrity of the person" might have universal appeal.

Numbers one and two are negative rights—freedom from restrictions. Number three is a positive right, freedom to have goods and services that are the basis for survival. It is necessary to include both positive and negative rights, for the definition must apply to people in different cultures and different economic circumstances. The right to life for many people means having food. There is little chance for universal support for human rights based only on Western civil liberties.

Positive economic rights are new. They arose in the twentieth century when economic development made it possible to distribute a minimum standard of living to everyone. Such entitlements become visible as government becomes more capable of guiding economic production and distribution, therefore more responsible for economic results.

Nations with relatively conservative ideologies, such as the United States, have been the least willing to emphasize positive rights, because of the widespread belief that people get what they deserve by competing in the marketplace. Conservatives are strong on negative rights and weak on positive rights.

In Northern Europe, countries with democratic socialism or welfare capitalism are likely to accept both positive and negative rights. Communist countries would be strongest on positive rights, largely economic rights, and weakest on negative rights, such as civil liberties. A fascist country such as South Africa would be the least likely to accept any form of human rights, because fascism requires belief in the superiority and privilege of the dominant group. The freedom, autonomy, and sovereignty of a *nation*—not the rights of people—would be supported, for the nation state and its controlling oligarchy is supreme within a fascist ideology.

ENVIRONMENTAL RIGHTS

At the outset in the development of the meaning of rights negative freedom was central. Then economic and political entitlements were added. Now we are beginning to include environmental rights. Environmental rights apply to health based on physical qualities such as air, water, food, and sound, and claims on resources, especially nonrenewable resources.

Environmental *rights* must be distinguished from environmental *permission*. This distinction can be illustrated as follows:

If a group of people attend a meeting held in one room and someone wants to smoke, the options include:

1. Having no rules and therefore allowing smokers to pollute the air nonsmokers must breathe (which implicitly provides rights to smokers but not nonsmokers).

2. Having a vote by which the majority rules.

3. Having a decision based on the personal preference of the leader.

4. Having a prohibition on smoking if there is even *one* person who does not smoke.

The first option constitutes environmental *laissez-faire*; the environment can be degraded by anyone. The second option constitutes environmental democracy, in which the majority rules without rights for minorities. The third option constitutes autocracy, in which the arbitrary preference of the leader produces the rule. *The fourth option is the only one involving environmental rights.*

Under a system of environmental rights, the smoker does not have an equal "right" to pollute. The breathing person has prior claim to a clean and healthful environment. The relationship between the smoker and nonsmoker is *not* considered symmetrical; each does not have the same claim to his personal preferences, for nonsmokers do not degrade the environment of smokers but smokers do degrade the environment of nonsmokers. If accommodation is made through separate smoking and nonsmoking areas, smokers should pay for added costs.

The nonsmokers' rights might also be supported by traditional concepts such as the "right" to privacy, or the "right" to life. But polluters, smoking persons, or smoke-producing factories have gone so far toward threatening the environmental rights of other people that such statements as the "right to clean and healthful environment" have become provisions in the state constitutions of Hawaii and Michigan. The explicit legal creation of environmental rights gives a person *prior* claim over industrial activities, whereas pollution during construction or operation of industry or business has often been treated as a "right" of the polluter. Many statutory restrictions on pollution have developed, some strong, some weak, some enforced, some unenforced, but constitutional rights are *meta-law*, producing superceding claims over statutory law or administrative actions. A citizen does not need to form a majority constituency to enforce an environmental claim if he has environmental rights as a citizen. By himself, the citizen can get courts to issue an injunction against the polluter if the air the person breathes is being polluted.

The hierarchical nature of rights over privilege is important because it is commonplace under liberal capitalism to treat cost-benefit analysis either as economic or to treat all costs and benefits as politically equal. There are economic costs to such rights as a clean and healthful environment, but if clean air and water are prior rights, these economic costs become expected costs of production. They are borne by the producer and passed on to the consumer of the specific product. To release pollutants into the air with costs placed on the general public is to subsidize private production by having the public (involuntarily) assume part of the cost of production. It is economic-environmental *laissez-faire* rather than planned economic production in which there are social priorities that have a higher value than economic production and profit making.

Prior environmental rights force the burden of proof onto the polluter. The citizen does not have to prove the air is dangerous; the polluter has to prove it is safe. In the battle over application of pesticides on forests there is an area of uncertainty about effects. The chemical companies have currently been unable to show that the pesticides are really safe. The public drinking water from the sprayed watershed has often not been proven conclusively to be endangered. In such cases, the public would probably not have pesticide in the water if the forest service and chemical companies were not allowed to use the material until the activity was shown to be safe. *With prior rights the appropriate method is that the "burden of proof" should fall on the possible polluter.* Without prior rights there will either be the use of the "preponderance of evidence" criterion, permitting the polluter to proceed if evidence one way or the other is not conclusive, or there is economic *laissez-faire* in which individual profit making is the only value.

When we have environmental rights, there is no longer choice on the part of an individual or corporation as to whether to pollute. That freedom has been restricted so that people have the freedom to breathe, to drink clean water, and to be protected from noise. Freedom for the polluter is slavery for the nonpolluter. It is no more "undemocratic" to take away the freedom to pollute than it is to take away the freedom to kill someone. Environmental rights restrict freedom of choice to nonpolluting options.

Total nonpollution would in most cases be an extreme and perhaps impossible goal. Political considerations require identification of the level of pollution the biosphere could carry without injury to human health and normal esthetic standards. For instance, those who wish to introduce chemicals into the environment should be required to prove that the quality of the environment and its cleanness and healthfulness would not be degraded. Some rivers, rich in bacteria, can absorb (eat) various materials without degradation of the normal ecosystem. Other rivers with pristine water may have no defenses against any additions.

Resource Rights

Another kind of environmental right is based on everyone's claim as a member of the human race to certain scarce resources, primarily those that are nonrenewable. This "common heritage" principle has been given special legitimacy in the Third United Nations Conference on the Law of the Seas, concluded in December, 1982.[4] When a resource is renewable but scarce, as are migratory ocean fish, it is part of the common heritage and should be shared *equitably*.

If resources are nonrenewable, there is not only a sharing obligation but also a nonconsumption obligation. For example, if copper is consumed by eventually going into dumps, it cannot be used by others. But if we use it so that it can later be recycled, we preserve the rights of future generations to its perpetual use. Changing from *consumption* to *use* is a movement from short-term objectives to long-term objectives, one which alters the nature of resource ownership rights.

Human rights to nonrenewable resources apply also to such scarce and irreplaceable resources as prime wilderness and natural beauty. Parks such as Yosemite, Grand Canyon, and Yellowstone give recognition to this right. These places do have other possible economic uses, but do we really want to mine Yosemite, or use it as a solid waste disposal dump? And, it is true that old-growth redwood makes good fences. The choice is ours: Should we preserve these remnants of ancient forests to be experienced by future generations or should we allow them to disappear in a few years in the wood of rotted fences, demarcating our suburban backyards?

If prime topsoil were classified as a largely nonrenewable resource, it would not ordinarily be converted to urban use. Neither would it be owned without restrictions preventing farmers from consuming it by misuse. Farming would only permit use rather than consumption (depletion) of prime topsoil. Because topsoil grows not only food but trees, forest practices that degrade topsoil would also be illegal. The topsoil would be in the public domain, part of the common heritage, and future generations would have a right to its perpetual use.

The global implications of the common heritage principle would mean that people in one country would not have the right to destroy "their" nonrenewable resources. Certain scarce renewable resources such as migratory ocean fish that are not owned by a particular nation would be prime candidates for common heritage claims. Legal and regulatory bodies would need to face up to such questions as: To whom should fishing rights belong? How heavily should these populations of fish be fished? Who has claim to the profits? A proposal that persists is to have an ocean regime that uses profits from ocean resources to aid the poor countries and help redress global economic inequalities without direct taxation of rich countries.

Realization of twenty-first century resource rights will require a new way of thinking about rights and will require new agreements, legal principles, and institutions to enforce such rights. Transition planning is now needed to augment work being done on laws of the oceans to include change in the definition of property rights. However, these redefinitions are not as drastic or unprecedented as they may seem, for property rights have not hitherto been absolute, as some people believe. For example, people own land only when they pay taxes on it. They cannot always do exactly what they wish with it, and it can be confiscated under rights of eminent domain. Nonetheless converting ownership of scarce resources from consumption rights to use rights and respecting claims on resources by the poor and the weak would open the way to considerable change in the twenty-first century.

Human Rights and Pluralism

Cultural and national variety has been accepted in the twentieth century to make pluralism the most popular social theory. But human rights transcend pluralism; when there is a conflict between group standards and human rights, group standards must yield. Otherwise, human rights have no real meaning, for the mores and beliefs of groups will be the ultimate standard instead of human rights. The basic question is whether what is practiced by groups will be accepted as right or whether universal standards of human rights will be used to *evaluate* and change the practices of groups, institutions, and nations. If group standards are increasingly based on rights we have universal progress.

Racism, for example, is practiced by many groups and nations, but does the practice legitimize racism? If rights of people are based on the worth and dignity of all people, then group practices should not be considered right merely because they are practiced. Neither should individuals be presumed to *be* right even though they have a "right" to *express* their opinion. If their opinion urges that other people be deprived of their basic rights as human beings, their opinions should *not* be respected.

Tolerance without ethical standards underlies this problem. In many respects the development of tolerance has been a twentieth century achievement, challenging the narrow-minded absolutism of cultures and religions that were permeated with prejudice. Anthropologists such as Ruth Benedict (*Patterns of Culture*) popularized "cultural relativism" and helped people break away from the notion that "our way is the right way." With no universal standards it is easy to conclude, then, that "their way is the right way for them." But what if "their way" denies human rights? Should our tolerance of "their way" accept *intolerance* of human rights if their way involves racism or any other denial of basic human rights?[5]

If what *is* triumphs over what *ought to be*, established practices are self-validating—whatever is, is right. The past and the present take priority over planning for a future that should respect common humanity.

We know that some cultures treat men as superior to women and are exploitive of women. Some nations treat entire racial groups as inferior and subject them to second-class status. Ancient cultures called for human sacrifices. Greek culture authorized chattel slavery. Since culture is, in fact, the cumulative habits and values of a group, it is an error to give ethical sanction to culture. Ethics and mores are *not* the same.

Nations, religious, and ethnic groups often use pluralist ideology as a way to keep the dominant group dominant. *An expanding system of legitimate world law would limit* the power of nations and subgroups that exceed human rights principles. If such world law is not based on human rights principles it could stamp out diversity in the name of universal standards. Diversity and pluralism in art, ideas, clothing, and lifestyles should be encouraged to make life more interesting and progressive, providing such diversity does not conflict with human rights. The Ku Klux Klan and the Nazis may expect their particular "lifestyle" to be tolerated even when it practices racism, but such a concession destroys the foundation of human rights.

The most dangerous current form of pluralism is unlimited national sovereignty. Nations have the power to produce genocide through nuclear war. So world law supporting human rights under a limited world government is essential for the realization of enforceable human rights, including the right to life. But decentralization has considerable value in stimulating progress in art, religion, lifestyles, and ideas. Variety within a system of universal rights should be the goal.

Violence Versus Human Rights

Much of the violence in the world is based either on structural exploitation, where one group has unfair power over another, or on counter violence, where the exploited group retaliates. Resistance to colonial power resulted in many of the revolutions since World War II, and we see revolution continuing or threatening to break out in many parts of the world. The Vietnam War was an example of indigenous reaction to colonial violence and exploitation. Central and South American revolutions feed on oligarchy that preserves extremes in wealth and power.

In such cases, human rights are denied by the forces of domination and claimed by the revolutionary groups. The danger is that means will become ends and that revolutionary groups will reinstate violence in the name of human rights. Yet when no nonviolent alternatives are available, armed liberation movements become the only hope against tyranny. The various forms of violence will be controlled only when real human rights are guaranteed through enforceable law.

There is understandable resistance to human rights achievements, for dominating groups fear the loss of advantages they now have. Many whites who had much higher incomes than blacks saw threats in "one person one vote" legislation. Men who dominate corporate executive power may see threats in women's liberation and the ERA. Rich nations see threats in human rights which give to Third World nations economic and political power that could result in more control over multinational corporations and produce higher labor costs. In a world in which people are often without entitlements as human beings but are bought and sold as grist for the economic mill, any movement toward human rights means that advantages will be lost by one group as another gains.

Yet human rights achievements are crucial to the future development of human community. We can choose to move toward guns, fences, police, terrorism, and fear—or toward social organization with principles of order based on high levels of community, cooperation, communication, and trust.

Design of twenty-first century human rights goals and the steps to achieve the transition constitutes a civilized revolution.

Rights achievements do not have to advance on all fronts at the same time. Perhaps we could first grant everyone a right to clean air and clean water; then, as a next step, the focus could be on equal pay for equal work, then on rights to employment, then on rights to be employed at a living wage, and later, the right to be employed at a living wage in environmentally responsible work.

Though advances will no doubt be uneven because different countries have different starting points, we must have intentional global planning with human rights objectives that are the same worldwide.

The ultimate violence of global nuclear war remains, however, our most urgent issue, for all other achievements in human rights would be canceled with global genocide. It is not true that if we have social justice within nations we will not have war between nations. In this nuclear age the threat of that ultimate violence means that war prevention is the first goal, the one that makes all other achievements possible. The route to global social justice must be achieved on a slower time schedule, but without unnecessary delay.

The "just war" theory is therefore obsolete. Because war in the nuclear age is the overriding enemy, other ways to achieve justice than through war must be found. This will entail a global system of reasonably just laws and enforcement processes under which we will be able to settle international disputes. The current structure of the world system now assures human genocide through nuclear war and also assures that the structural violence based on exploitation of the weak by the powerful will predominate over human rights.

Rights Versus Voluntarism

Voluntary support of human rights, while helpful, is not a sufficient procedure for realizing them. We need both a widespread belief in human rights and also acceptance of the legitimacy of *enforced compliance*. If local governments could choose whether they supported freedom of religion and the press, the Bill of Rights would have died long ago.

Voluntarism also has its limits in the marketplace. In the early 1970s *Fortune* conducted a survey of heads of major corporations to ask whether their company produced air or water pollution. Most said yes and also agreed that it was not good for the society. When asked if they would voluntarily control their pollution, they said no. When asked if they would accept federal regulation, most said *yes*.

Voluntary compliance in a market system would put those who comply at a competitive disadvantage and reduce their profits. Uniform compliance, which would have to be enforced, would permit all companies to pass on pollution control costs to consumers and would produce no disadvantage in profits or competitive pricing. The rules of the economic structure largely determine the outcome.

Human rights are crippled if compliance is a matter of choice on the part of nations, for rights are then secondary to national power. A universal standard of human rights should stand in the same relationship to nations as the American Constitution does to states. *A global human rights constitution will therefore be necessary to supersede national governments in the area of human rights.*

The Universal Declaration of Human Rights was an attempt by the UN to formulate supranational standards prior to the creation of an enforcement mechanism. We must now create world law with enforcement power, if human rights are to go beyond the values of the current system, which permit *voluntary* national compliance.

Human Rights and Human Responsibilities

Some human rights are gained at the expense of loss to others. Ordinarily, the right to free speech when used by one person would not produce a loss to another, for words are part of an economy of abundance, especially when their transmission does not require scarce resources such as wood for paper. Although electronic communication and speech in a public meeting have the possibility of largely unlimited expression of speech, electronic communication does involve capital costs and energy. Speech in a public meeting also occurs within a time span during which domination by a few can be at the expense of others. But compared to a "right to shelter" involving land, labor, and materials, the right to free speech requires less sacrifice by some in order to support the rights of all.

If economic rights entitle some people to food and shelter without their being obligated to contribute to the economy, other people are supporting those rights through *their* labor. Unfairness then develops in the name of rights. Therefore, if a person is mentally and physically capable of contributing to an economy, any economic *entitlement* also requires personal contribution *obligations*, for an economy is based on the labor of its members.

Similar obligations arise when people do not want to work but yet want to receive unemployment checks, and when, in a world where land is a scarce resource, they want land but want no land use planning.

What standards of obligation and entitlement should be used for implementing the food, medicine, and shelter rights of the world's people? Should the total world economy and the global carrying capacity be the standard for fair entitlement, or should standards vary on the basis of nations and customs?

The concept of "entitlement" was redefined under the Reagan administration ideology to mean mainly "what you can get" under conditions of market capitalism. The presumption of open markets is applicable, however, only to part of the world system; the real world is heavily controlled by other forms of power, visible in OPEC, Western multinationals, and the military-economic-political power of industrial nations. The modern world is largely an oligarchy of the rich and the powerful, rather than either an open competitive market or an ethical system based on human rights.

Rights and obligations become additionally complicated with respect to population and resource carrying capacity. If a poor country has a maximum population in relation to its food production capacity, and if it fails to control its population, should other countries provide food if the poor country cannot pay for it? Should the supplying of food be tagged with birth control obligations? The right to life is at stake, yet uncontrolled population also jeopardizes the right to life. *Does the poor country have an obligation to the larger world society to control its local population if the larger world society is to respect its need for food?*

Consider, on the other hand, the rich nations, where consumption levels rather than population numbers pose a similar problem. If the United States consumes more energy than it can create within its borders and thus draws on nonrenewable resources such as petroleum from other parts of the world, should the wasteful American "standard of living" be accepted by the world community or should it be regarded as a threat to people's basic needs to have fuel for cooking and keeping warm? Should the poor nations expect the United States to control its over-consumption if the United States is to expect cooperation from the poor nations? Should luxuries in the United States take priority over needs elsewhere so basic they involve the right to life?

Here again we have a conflict between ethics of rights and obligations on one hand and the exercise of power on the other. In the twenty-first century we will need to emphasize human rights over consumption excesses and population excesses if the "common heritage" is to be used on an equitable world basis. Otherwise, human rights will be denied. Without progress in rights, conflict, including violent conflict, could characterize the twenty-first century.

TRANSITION STEPS

The first step in transition requires education and dialogue. Schools, churches, businesses, unions, and the media must engage in a public examination of the philosophical and practical aspects of human rights. A country such as the United States, with its strong religious and humanist traditions relating to belief in "the worth and dignity of the human person," should be in a good position to carry on public dialogue on the implications of human rights and the changes needed to permit their realization.

If the human person is the locus of value, how legitmate is the demand of a nation that its soldiers kill people in another country? Only if the killing is really "defense" against an invader, who is, in effect, a murderer, do arms become real national *defense*. Military actions are seldom of this type. The Vietnam War is a case in point.

In fact, the American govenment did not even try to claim that American military action in Vietnam was a matter of American defense. Rather, it was said to be in the American "interest" and within the SEATO treaty.[6] What this meant was that American soldiers were supposed to kill people in another country to serve American foreign policy as created by the President.

If we believe in *human* rights to life, American action consisted of Americans committing murder. The word "murder" has a moral connotation different from "killing," which is merely a description of an act without judgment attached. In a future in which human rights are supreme, any act of killing anyone in or out of one's country, when not in self-defense, would be morally classified as "murder" and the corresponding legal classification would follow.

To be more precise—if there are to be *human* rights, acts such as those of American soldiers in Vietnam or Soviet soldiers in Afghanistan, involving killing or "hiring" killers—would be tried by either a national or international court, and would be treated as criminal acts of murder, much as if we were dealing with soldiers in the American Air Force who had bombed and strafed Los Angeles.

This pre-human rights world we live in confines law to nations. It is a "nation's rights" world, not a "human rights" world. Those who have power over national action and policy can nullify the basic human rights of thousands or even millions of other people by depriving them of life. Further, national law will typically support such action. If we are to see an affirmation of basic human rights in the twenty-first century, there is a long way to go. The first step involves changes in the minds of people, but the most formidable step will be the creation of new political structures.

We must reevaluate current laws and politics and create new law where it is needed to serve human rights. The most obvious vacuum is in world law, of course, but there must also be major changes in national constitutional law, extending human rights within countries.

Next should come the specific transition planning with a scheduled phasing in of human rights, taking account of strategies to make the changes as acceptable as possible. A good procedure would begin with identifying minimal objectives and maximal objectives, noting where nations already stand in relation to human rights progress. Simultaneously, there should be worldwide participation in the planning of these minimal objectives and long-range maximal goals, and of the timetable as well. Transformation will occur when the goals move from the minds of people into a specific institutional transition plan.

Neither the poor nations nor the rich are centrally concerned with each other's survival needs; therefore, political cooperation requires combining mutual concerns, e.g., linking food for poor nations with war prevention for the rich. The "right to life" has a different context in different parts of the world, and global transition steps must take these differences into account.

The most plausible plan, therefore, would be based on gaining widespread acceptance of certain values as explicit goals and then getting contextual application of those values in nations and regions. For instance, if value priorities were (1) survival, (2) social justice, and (3) quality of life, these values could be given meaning according to the way they are interpreted in different parts of the world, providing these local interpretations did not violate the rights of people.

Transition planning then requires decisions on short-range and long-range goals which can be also interpreted as minimal and maximal objectives. Minimal objectives are the *most urgent*, the ones which produce severe consequences for the future if action is not taken. They are *not* the most *expedient*. They also consist of actions consistent with long-range objectives. The following outline represents an example.

Outline of a Transition Model: Human Rights

	Minimal (Short Goals)	*Maximal (21st Century)*
Global:	Minimum nutrition	Full employment opportunities at
	Clean water	a fair wage in socially useful, en-
	Shelter	vironmentally responsible work.

	Minimal (Short Goals)	Maximal (21st Century)
		Equal economic conditions. for groups, regardless of sex, race, ethnicity.
	Freedom from torture	
	Freedom from murder	
	Participation in public policy	Steady-state economics based on incoming energy and sustainable resources.
	Employment	
		Abolition of military systems; world law, collective police force.

National:

1. United States	Right to employment Clean and healthful environment Equal opportunity on basis of sex, race, ethnicity Preservation of nonrenewable resources for future generations Traditional civil liberties	Same as above
2. Other nations	(Determined contextually)	Same as above

Demands for human rights will have to start with local movements before they are accepted at a national or global level, and difficult struggles may occur at every step along the way. It was only after a difficult and even violent struggle that the civil rights movement broke through the power of racists and sexists. Even now racial and sexual rights have been only partially won in the United States, but a worldwide movement is also underway that will be hard to stop.

New gains are being made daily in environmental rights. People are demanding that restaurants, public buildings, and workplaces treat smoking as a privilege, the breathing of clean air as a right. Progressive areas such as San Francisco, Oregon, and Hawaii have taken legal steps to protect the nonsmoker from the pollution of the smoker. Smoke, noise, and ugliness of environment should be considered a form of exploitation that is no longer tolerable. Laws have begun to protect people's "right" to the sun, a principle established in Japan, to ensure that houses using solar collectors will have a right to continued unobstructed sunlight. The high rises of cities have for years stolen the light of others without compensation.

Transnational groups such as churches, unions, scholarly organizations, and anti-war groups are likely to spearhead global implementation of human rights. But even the lip service progressive nations and decision makers give to human rights helps to legitimize the movement and strengthen it to challenge the structure of privilege. One or two universally supported rights may be the first to become enforceable, preparing the way for others.

War prevention needs to be the first goal, because the right to life and the rights of future generations currently are threatened by the present nuclear war system. A strengthened World Court, a world security council, and a standing world police force would form the basic elements of a supranational system of law, expandable to serve other rights such as rights to food and a livable environment.

Human rights guarantees would create a new ethical level in human evolution, promoting foundations for world community and world civilization. When those who want human rights for ethical and humanitarian reasons, those who want rights because they no longer will accept repression, and those who see certain rights as essential to the continuation of the human race combine forces, they will become formidable political allies. If we can thus lay the groundwork for human rights by the end of this century, the twenty-first century can be the time of expansion and flowering of social values and law. Otherwise, if progress is not made, the twenty-first century will probably be precarious and violent, possibly terminating the continuation of the human race.

Universal Declaration of Human Rights
(Adopted on December 10th, 1948 by General Assembly of United Nations at the Palais de Chaillot, Paris)

Whereas Member States have pledged themselves to achieve, in co-operation with the United Nations, the promotion of universal respect for and observance of human rights and fundamental freedoms,

Whereas a common understanding of these rights and freedoms is of the greatest importance for the full realization of this pledge,

Now, therefore, the General Assembly, Proclaim this Universal Declaration of Human Rights as a common standard of achievement for all peoples and all nations, to the end that every individual and every organ of society, keeping this Declaration constantly in mind, shall strive by teaching and education to promote respect for these rights and freedoms and by progressive measures, national and international, to secure their universal and effective recognition and observance, both among the peoples of Member States themselves and among the peoples of territories under their jurisdiction.

Article 1

All human beings are born free and equal in dignity and rights. They are endowed with reason and conscience and should act towards one another in a spirit of brotherhood.

Article 2

1. Everyone is entitled to all the rights and freedoms set forth in this Declaration, without distinction of any kind, such as race, colour, sex, language, religion, political or other opinion, national or social origin, property, birth or other status.

2. Furthermore, no distinction shall be made on the basis of the political, jurisdictional or international status of the country or territory to which a person belongs, whether it be independent, trust, non-self-governing or under any other limitation of sovereignty.

Article 3

Everyone has the right to life, liberty and security of person.

Article 4

No one shall be held in slavery or servitude; slavery and the slave trade shall be prohibited in all their forms.

Article 5

No one shall be subjected to torture or to cruel, inhuman or degrading treatment or punishment.

Article 6

Everyone has the right to recognition everywhere as a person before the law.

Article 7

All are equal before the law and are entitled without any discrimination to equal protection of the law. All are entitled to equal protection against any discrimination in violation of this Declaration and against any incitement to such discrimination.

Article 8

Everyone has the right to an effective remedy by the competent national tribunals for acts violating the fundamental rights granted him by the constitution or by law.

Article 9

No one shall be subjected to arbitrary arrest, detention or exile.

Article 10

Everyone is entitled to full equality to a fair and public hearing by an independent and impartial tribunal, in the determination of his rights and obligations and of any criminal charge against him.

Article 11

1. Everyone charged with a penal offence has the right to be presumed innocent until proved guilty according to law in a public trial at which he has had all the guarantees necessary for his defence.

2. No one shall be held guilty of any penal offence on account of any act or omission which did not constitute a penal offence, under national or international law, at the time when it was committed. Nor shall a heavier penalty be imposed than the one that was applicable at the time the penal offence was committed.

Article 12

No one shall be subjected to arbitrary interference with his privacy, family, home or correspondence, nor to attacks upon his honour and reputation. Everyone has the right to the protection of the law against such interference or attacks.

Article 13

1. Everyone has the right to freedom of movement and residence within the borders of each State.

2. Everyone has the right to leave any country, including his own, and to return to his country.

Article 14

1. Everyone has the right to seek and to enjoy in other countries asylum from persecution.

2. This right may not be invoked in the case of prosecutions genuinely arising from non-political crimes or from acts contrary to the purposes and principles of the United Nations.

Article 15

1. Everyone has the right to a nationality.

2. No one shall be arbitrarily deprived of his nationality nor denied the right to change his nationality.

Article 16

1. Men and women of full age, without any limitation due to race, nationality or religion, have the right to marry and to found a family. They are entitled to equal rights as to marriage, during marriage and at its dissolution.
2. Marriage shall be entered into only with the free and full consent of the intending spouses.
3. The family is the natural and fundamental group unit of society and is entitled to protection by society and the State.

Article 17

1. Everyone has the right to own property alone as well as in association with others.
2. No one shall be arbitrarily deprived of his property.

Article 18

Everyone has the right to freedom of thought, conscience and religion; this right includes freedom to change his religion or belief, and freedom, either alone or in community with others and in public or private, to manifest his religion or belief in teaching, practice, worship and observance.

Article 19

Everyone has the right to freedom of opinion and expression; this right includes freedom to hold opinions without interference and to seek, receive and impart information and ideas through any media and regardless of frontiers.

Article 20

1. Everyone has the right to freedom of peaceful assembly and association.
2. No one may be compelled to belong to an association.

Article 21

1. Everyone has the right to take part in the government of his country, directly or through freely chosen representatives.
2. Everyone has the right of equal access to public service in his country.
3. The will of the people shall be the basis of the authority of government; this will shall be expressed in periodic and genuine elections which shall be by universal and equal suffrage and shall be held by secret vote or by equivalent free voting procedures.

Article 22

Everyone, as a member of society, has the right to social security and is entitled to realization, through national effort and international co-operation and in accordance with the organization and resources of each State, of the economic, social and cultural rights indispensable for his dignity and the free development of his personality.

Article 23

1.   Everyone has the right to work, to free choice of employment, to just and favourable conditions of work and to protection against unemployment.

2.   Everyone, without any discrimination, has the right to equal pay for equal work.

3.   Everyone who works has the right to just and favourable remuneration ensuring for himself and his family an existence worthy of human dignity, and supplemented, if necessary, by other means of social protection.

4.   Everyone has the right to form and to join trade unions for the protection of his interests.

Article 24

Everyone has the right to rest and leisure, including reasonable limitation of working hours and periodic holidays with pay.

Article 25

1.   Everyone has the right to a standard of living adequate for the health and well-being of himself and of his family, including food, clothing, housing and medical care and necessary social services, and the right to security in the event of unemployment, sickness, disability, widowhood, old age or other lack of livelihood in circumstances beyond his control.

2.   Motherhood and childhood are entitled to special care and assistance. All children, whether born in or out of wedlock, shall enjoy the same social protection.

Article 26

1.   Everyone has the right to education. Education shall be free, at least in the elementary and fundamental stages. Elementary education shall be compulsory. Technical and professional education shall be made generally available and higher education shall be equally accessible to all on the basis of merit.

2.   Education shall be directed to the full development of the human personality and to the strengthening of respect for human rights and fundamental freedoms. It shall promote understanding, tolerance and friendship among all nations, racial or religious groups, and shall further the activities of the United Nations for the maintenance of peace.

3.   Parents have a prior right to choose the kind of education that shall be given to their children.

Article 27

1.   Everyone has the right freely to participate in the cultural life of the community, to enjoy the arts and to share in scientific advancement and its benefits.

2.   Everyone has the right to the protection of the moral and material interests resulting from any scientific, literary or artistic production of which he is the author.

Article 28

Everyone is entitled to a social and international order in which the rights and freedoms set forth in this Declaration shall be fully realised.

1.   Everyone has duties to the community in which alone the free and full development of his personality is possible.

2.   In the exercise of his rights and freedoms, everyone shall be subject only to such limitations as are determined by law solely for the purpose of securing due recognition and respect for the rights and freedoms of others and of meeting the just requirements of morality, public order and the general welfare in a democratic society.

3.   These rights and freedoms may in no case be exercised contrary to the purposes and principles of the United Nations.

Article 30

Nothing in this Declaration may be interpreted as implying for any State, group or person any right to engage in any activity or to perform any act aimed at the destruction of any of the rights and freedoms set forth herein.

NOTES

1. Arthur Schlesinger, Jr., "Human Rights and the American Tradition," *Foreign Affairs—America and the World 1978* (Council on Foreign Relations, Vol. 57, No. 3, 1979), pp. 503–26.

2. For a history of the Universal Declaration see: Egon Schwelb, *Human Rights and International Community* (New York: Quadrangle Books, 1964).

3. Schlesinger, Jr., "Human Rights and the American Tradition," p. 515.

4. William Wertenbaker, "A Reporter at Large: Law of the Seas Conference Part II," *New Yorker* (August 8, 1983), p. 56.

5. Robert Wolff, Barrington Moore, Jr., and Herbert Marcuse, *A Critique of Pure Tolerance* (Boston: Beacon Press, 1969).

6. Telford Taylor, *Nuremberg and Vietnam: An American Tragedy* (New York: Bantam Books, 1970), pp 106–08.

SELECTED READINGS

Ajami, Fouad. 1978. *Human Rights and World Order Politics*. New York: Institute for World Order, Working Papers No. 4.

Brown, Peter and Douglas MacLean. 1979. *Human Rights and U.S. Foreign Policy, Principles and Applications*. Lexington, Massachusetts: Lexington.

Cranston, Maurice. 1978. *What Are Human Rights?* New York: Taplinger.

Dominguez, Jorge, et al. 1979. *Enhancing Global Human Rights*. New York: McGraw-Hill.

Joyce, James. 1979. *The New Politics of Human Rights*. New York: St. Martin's.

Kothari, Rajni. 1980. *Toward a Just World*. New York: Institute for World Order, Working Papers No. 11.

Melden, A. I. 1970. *Human Rights*. Belmont, California: Wadsworth.

Mendlovitz, Saul H., ed. 1975. *On the Creation of a Just World Order: Preferred Worlds for the 1990s*. New York: The Free Press.

Miller, William. 1977. *International Human Rights: A Bibliography, 1870–1976*. Notre Dame, Indiana: University of Notre Dame Law School.

Newberg, Paula, ed. 1980. *The Politics of Human Rights*. New York: New York University.

Said, Abdul Aziz, ed. 1978. *Human Rights and World Order*. New York: Praeger.

Schwelb, Egon. 1964. *Human Rights and the International Community*. Chicago, Illinois: Quadrangle Books.

Thompson, Kenneth. 1980. *The Moral Imperative of Human Rights: A World Survey*. Lanham, Maryland: University Press of America.

3

Energy:
Transition from
the Petroleum Era

The modern world is built on energy slaves, machines that greatly multiply the energy of human labor. Our transportation, manufacturing, communication, home comforts, and conveniences are based on energy and technology. The most useful and convenient form of energy has been petroleum, because it is easy to transport, relatively clean, and until recently, very accessible.

But accessible petroleum is being rapidly depleted, and we must move to other forms of energy. This transition will produce profound changes in our transportation, our production, our architecture, the costs of heat and power, and our habit of wasting energy.

SOURCES OF ENERGY

All energy is ultimately either nuclear or gravitational. The sun produces its heat through nuclear energy. It heats the earth and that heat is captured mainly through photosynthesis in plants. Insects and animals eat plants and are therefore fueled by solar energy. As geological changes occurred in the past, the fossils of plants and animals and their decay products produced petroleum, coal, natural gas, and similar deposits. These fossil sources are finite in amount and not renewable in any foreseeable geological future. Gravitational energy holds the planets in a near circular pattern, energy inertia moves the earth, and gravitation makes the oceans rise and fall. This tidal energy can be captured and used. But solar energy is overwhelmingly the most significant source for our use.

The sun both "giveth and taketh away," for it also produces deadly radiation which is, however, sufficiently screened by the atmosphere and ionosphere to keep cell destruction at a low level and permit animal life. The cumulative destruction of cells eventually determines a maximum life span. When man replicates the sun by creating nuclear energy on earth, the natural process by which the sun retains its radioactive waste does not occur; neither is radiation filtered by the atmosphere. Serious problems arise that have not been solved and may, in fact, be unsolvable. Man-made nuclear energy could be the fatal, final polluter of the planet. The use of solar energy avoids these consequences.

There are many forms of solar energy. Direct solar energy is heat which warms the air and heats the ground, our bodies, and our buildings. Indirect solar energy is derived from fossil fuel, wood, wind, rain-river-hydroelectric power, food from plants, food from animals, and ocean temperature differentials. Fossil fuels are finite and nonrenewable. Solar energy is incoming and renewable. Knowing this much provides the basis for the general structure of energy transition planning, for solar energy is sustainable and fossil fuels are not.

TRANSITION STRATEGY

The only long-run future that makes sense is one in which we make direct and indirect use of continuous, renewable, solar energy. But how much time have we in the short run to continue using fossil fuels and nuclear power? Let us first explore the nuclear alternative.

Nuclear fission, which nuclear power plants use, is based on finite sources of uranium. The process creates disposal dangers from spent uranium, which produces plutonium and a variety of radioactive isotopes with varying decay rates — some lasting 250,000 years. Plutonium decays 50 percent in 24,000 years. The economics of nuclear fission, its relatively short fuel life (a few decades), the decommissioning-dismantling costs, and its public health problems make it a high-risk energy source during transition because of the long pollution effects of radioactive waste. Radioactive pollution is an insidious destroyer of life, producing diseases such as leukemia.

Nuclear *fusion* is different. The sun's energy and the hydrogen bomb are based on fusion, which uses abundant light resources, highly available in ocean water. Fission uses heavy radioactive metals. Fusion brings light materials together and creates enormous temperatures, but under current technology the explosion lasts only a moment. If it could be sustained, it would probably melt any container.

Fusion produces much less radioactivity than fission and is based on very abundant resources, but its economic and technical feasibility is still speculative. Because it is so uncertain, it would be dangerous to rely on fusion in planning the future. Even considering the most technologically optimistic fusion future, we must remember that an energy source that is out of balance with the earth's ecosystem, adding heat from a source other than the sun, will heat the atmosphere. Global thermopollution is very dangerous, affecting weather, rainfall, polar ice, ocean levels, and food sources.

But if nuclear fission is clearly dangerous and finite, and nuclear fusion is somewhat dangerous and speculative, how much time have we in the short run to continue using fossil fuels?

The answer is: Not much time for petroleum, possibly 20 to 50 years, somewhat more for natural gas, and considerably more for coal.[1] Researchers believe world oil production will level off as early as 1985 or as late as the end of the century. It is difficult to make exact predictions, for this depends not only on accurate estimates of available resources but also on consumption levels. If consumption increases exponentially, time is very short, but decline in consumption would extend supply. Moreover, resources available at deep land and ocean levels may take more energy to extract than they would produce. The question is not merely whether the earth has a particular amount of fossil fuel but, beyond that, where is it and what are the costs of obtaining it?

Fossil fuels are distributed unevenly on the earth. In terms of geology, the United States was abundantly endowed, but we have exploited oil so rapidly that ours is the first oil supply to move toward exhaustion. The remaining petroleum to be found within the United States is scarce and deep. Drilling is producing many costly dry wells. It is expected that within a decade or so it will take as much energy to obtain oil as it produces. The cost of finding oil could exceed the value of the oil itself.

Other areas of the world still have substantial reserves, the Middle East being the area of largest known reserves. But global demand can exhaust these supplies by the early part of the twenty-first century, especially if Third World countries move toward the high consumption patterns of industrial nations. The Workshop on Alternative Energy Strategies, a two-and-a-half year international study completed in 1977, concluded that "the supply of oil will fail to meet increasing demand before the year 2,000, most probably between 1985 and 1995, even if energy prices rise 50 percent above current levels in real terms."[2] The current petroleum glut does not offset the long-term trend, for if supply is increased in the short run it will surely run out faster in the future. Whatever course is taken to provide an energy future for people on this planet, it will have to be based on the assumption that such a future cannot rely on petroleum, for though the end is not months or even years away, few machines of the twenty-first century will run on gasoline, kerosene, or any other petroleum-based product.

If we anticipate the transition, the trauma of conversion will be minimized. Transition from oil has already begun in minor ways, but the major transition must now be cooperatively planned in anticipation of lead times or else we will face economic and social disruption that could produce world hysteria, frantic stop-gap solutions, and competitive conflicts that could result in World War III.

Energy Costs

The word "cost" should refer to the full range of costs, not merely economic costs. Nuclear fission involves health and life costs of future generations. Petroleum involves air pollution costs. Coal involves even greater air and water pollution costs, including acid rain and, when underground mining is used, costs for the life and health of miners. Natural gas is less air polluting and has lower total health costs than other fossil fuels.

Hydroelectric costs involve other external costs. Cities, farmland, and forests may be inundated by dams, and migratory fish are often reduced or eliminated. The use of wood for energy can produce large amounts of air pollution, and excessive use depletes forests and is currently producing topsoil destruction and deserts, especially in tropical regions.

The complication and size of energy-producing technology, such as nuclear power plants or large ocean thermal energy conversion units, produce centralized control of energy and result in dependence on expensive high technology. Centralized control produces excessive political power on the part of a producer. Centralized energy sources usually make communities and nations vulnerable to sabotage, terrorism, and technological failures that can deprive large areas of energy.[3]

Economic costs become relative to each other. Is natural gas cheaper than coal? Is bio-gas cheaper than natural gas? Is nuclear fuel cheaper than hydroelectric? Are the costs only internal or also external? External costs would involve, for example, the health effects of burning coal, the money for medical care, the personal costs of a blighted environment, and the misery of sickness and death.

And what are the costs of decisions that exert veto power over future generations, either by depleting finite resources that are part of our common heritage or by leaving a radioactive legacy that adds to the sickness and cancer levels of future generations?

Treating energy costs as merely the short-term dollar return for dollars invested has been a colossal mistake. Costs can be internal and external, short term and long term; they can be economic, social, ethical, political, military, and ecological. The amount and the kind of employment and the general quality of life are tied to energy planning. Energy is integral to the full set of considerations that bear on the "good life" and the most feasible future for human beings. When single nations, corporations, or individuals make decisions without giving major weight to these larger ethical and long-term considerations, we have anarchistic, special interest, energy nonplanning. We now live in this kind of mutual self-defeating arrangement, where energy decisions by one group have high impact on another. Transition, therefore, requires not only technological solutions but educational, economic, and political solutions as well.

It is useful to have an overview of some of the basic economic sectors before developing transition policies.

Economic Sectors

Transportation

Movement of things and people accounts for over half of American petroleum consumption. Automobiles and trucks use about 75 percent of the transportation energy. Airplanes are the least efficient users of petroleum. Railways are the most efficient.

The American economy is the world's most automobile centered. Ours are larger, use more petroleum, and are driven farther each year. Futhermore, over 40 percent of the world's cars are in the United States, though we have only 6 percent of the world's population.

Trucking is the main method of moving goods, though it is less energy-efficient than train transportation. Because of the need for heavy-duty highways for trucks, road costs are far higher, and roads themselves in materials and construction fuel are high consumers of petroleum. In 1980 it cost about $50 million per mile to build a six-lane freeway, but for the two-way rail system from San Diego to Tijuana, construction costs were only $5 million per mile.

Road repairs are part of transportation costs. It is estimated that repair maintenance of American roads in the 1980s will cost $800 *billion*, about $16,000 for each family.[4]

When trains carry more and trucks carry less, fuel use and total economic costs will be substantially reduced.

Continued production of lighter and more fuel-efficient automobiles coupled with increases in the number of people riding per car, can significantly reduce fuel use. We can also conserve petroleum by increasing use of buses and trains for public transport.

We have already made some notable savings when some of us shifted from large gas-guzzling cars, though gas guzzlers continue to be manufactured and sold. A decline in airline travel has begun and is likely to continue with increased fuel costs. But the development of mass transit by bus and train lags sorely in the United States, where we are loath to unilaterally give up our individual personal vehicles. More safety needs to be built into lighter cars to attract buyers, though they become relatively more safe if there are fewer heavy cars to collide with in case of accidents.

Federal regulations on automobile manufacturers and higher fuel costs have both begun to have impact on automobile fuel consumption. But we must induce people to use alternative modes of transportation, such as bus and train, by making then both reliable and low in cost.[5]

Manufacturing

Heat energy and work energy from electric motors are the primary forms of industrial energy consumption. With the exception of such industries as aluminum extraction, heat energy usually comes from fossil fuel. Electric motors usually get their energy from fossil fuel generators and hydroelectric power. Most manufacturing is based on fossil fuel energy.

Some industries have begun to generate a portion of their own heat and electric power from their own combustible wastes. Excess electric generation has been produced in some industries by their "cogeneration," resulting in sales of electricity *into* the grid. Much European manufacturing is based on the use of smaller electric motors and newer ways to manufacture steel. As American industries begin to adopt the more efficient technologies of Europe, they can cut their petroleum, coal, gas, and hydroelectric consumption to a considerable degree.

The products which industry designs and manufactures are a substantial part of either the problem or the solution. We need to develop smaller, lighter, more durable products, less wastefully packaged, and requiring less energy in their production. Information to the consumer about product energy consumption helps to sell low-energy products. Considerable energy goes into the manufacture of an automobile, the dominant petroleum consumer, but the newer, lighter automobiles are costing less energy to manufacture.

Commercial Business

Most buildings are sieves that leak out heat in the winter and leak in heat in the summer. Better architecture would make more use of insulation and passive solar design to reflect and protect from heat in the summer and to absorb and hold solar heat in the winter.

Lighting in our commercial buildings is often excessive. Lights are left on all night in many large buildings for the convenience of cleaning crews. Buildings are overheated in the winter and overcooled in the summer. It is not uncommon for people working in business offices to wear sweaters in the summer because the air conditioning is too cold.

Supermarkets often use open frozen-food areas that allow cold air to spill out and require enormous, noisy refrigeration machines. Doors to businesses are often left open in the summer and winter while machines try to keep inside temperatures comfortable at the cost of great energy waste. These habits began in the cheap energy, cheap petroleum era and are being changed, but the rate of conserving energy can be greatly facilitated through retrofitting of old buildings and better design of new ones. High energy costs speed conversion, but waste has been encouraged in the past by pricing electricity and petroleum products for business so that the larger the consumption the smaller the unit cost. Heavy consumers, often with the planning of a Public Utilities Commission, have been charged rates that subsidize waste and discourage conservation. Changes in the rate curve are underway and could greatly facilitate changes in business practices.

Businesses require transportation for foods, employees, and customers. If we locate businesses close to customers and the the homes of employees, we can reduce energy consumption accordingly. In the past, planners have rarely considered energy cost-benefit advantages when choosing business locations. For example, shopping centers and decentralized offices in the community provide energy advantages plus employee and consumer convenience.

Shopping centers, however, are built around the automobile and reinforce the automobile economy. Reduced automobile and energy use will require shopping centers that make convenient use of mass transit and bicycles. In cities we will have to have shopping areas that exclude the automobile and require peripheral parking and convenient low-energy access from people's homes; many of these areas might be within walking distance.

If people make more use of their houses for their work, much transportation energy would be saved. If commuting is better organized through car pooling, three or four people can use the amount of energy one might use. By adding new technology, we can gain remarkable results. American cars during the 1960s and 1970s, for example, often got about 15 miles per gallon and were usually driven by one person, but cars now and in the future can easily get 35 to 45 miles per gallon. Four people in a 35-mile-per-gallon car get 140 miles per gallon per person. This is an increase of more than 900 percent in energy use efficiency, achieved only by *using current technology plus planned social cooperation.* The 45-mile-per-gallon car of the mid-1980s with four persons to the car will produce a 1,200 percent increase in miles per gallon per person. Even with one person in the car, a 45-mile-per-gallon car can achieve a 300 percent increase, which means that it is using one-third the fuel consumed by the old gas guzzler. And well-designed, light-rail public transport is even more efficient.

Moreover, when we begin to make more extensive use of the telephone, the computer, and the expanded consumer information increasingly available from TV, we will not have to make so many trips for researching and ordering consumer items.

Residential

Most houses leak heat in the winter and cool air in the summer. We can accomplish much to remedy this fact with new architecture and retrofit much older housing. We can plug cracks, incorporate better wall and ceiling insulation, install thermopane windows, build solar collectors for hot water, locate windows so that they will collect the heat from winter sun, and plant trees to provide shade in the summer.

In houses with high ceilings that collect the heat, slow-moving fans can force the heat down. Many houses can be cooled entirely by using basement air, which is cooled by the ground.

Heat pumps are much more efficient users of electric energy when electricity is the source of heat. Wood stoves are useful in rural areas where smoke can be dispersed and where wood is abundant. Wood stoves are useful for home heating, and with heating coils added, can heat water as well.

Many houses can use solar collectors, especially in cool, sunny areas. Solar plates can produce hot water and glassed-in solar sunspaces can capture large amounts of heat. Photo-voltaic cells are rapidly dropping in price and will soon be economical. Wind energy is promising for areas with prevailing winds. Residue from human and animal waste, combined with plant biomass, can produce bio-gas and methane, which can heat a house and be used for cooking in place of fossil-based propane and natural gas; houses of the future should not waste potential energy from septic tanks.

ENERGY AND LIFESTYLE

The previous suggestions involve possibilities for energy conservation based on technology. Technological changes can help the world shift away from oil dependency with little or no change in real lifestyle and "standard of living."

There is, however, a developing frontier in the way we define standard of living. Various consumer movements have begun which center on simple, low-energy consumption lifestyles. Among these changes are eating lower on the food chain, consuming less meat and saving the excess grains and other plants for food export and alcohol production. Alcohol could then fuel most small automobiles at prices not much different from current petroleum prices. In turn, the higher health level resulting from fewer heart attacks and lower incidence of cancer and diabetes would provide high energy savings and lower medical costs for the entire society.

Houses with better esthetic design but less space could be more easily heated. In addition, if people wore sweaters more often in the winter and held the house temperature down, they would increase their health level if the temperature reduction was not too great. The same "comfort" changes could occur in workplaces. In the past, houses and workplaces have often been overheated, causing discomfort to people not used to such high temperatures.

Hot water requires a major portion of household energy, and changes in bathing habits can significantly reduce energy consumption.

Bathtubs are often filled unnecessarily high with water that is too hot. If a bath is used for therapeutic or pleasure purposes, washing can be done in a shower ahead of time and the entire family can use the same bath water without the use of soap, a tradition in Japan. Bath heat can be put into the house by draining water when it cools. Similarly, use of the shower, which usually takes less hot water, can be kept to minimal water consumption by getting clean and getting out instead of standing under the shower for inordinate lengths of time.

Using cold-water soap in clothes washers is a considerable energy saver. Two other high energy users are clothes dryers and refrigerators. In the case of clothes dryers, we can when feasible shift to the famous economy solar dryer known as the "clothes line." Or, if we are using the clothes dryer, we might, in areas where humidity is low, make use of the waste heat to heat the house. Refrigerators have become loaded with complex "conveniences" that add to the original cost, require far more maintenance, reduce the life span of the appliance, and use much more electricity. The more simple and basic the refrigerator, without automatic ice-makers and automatic defrost, the lower the energy consumption. Such changes in lifestyle are away from the increasingly complicated technology that has usually ignored energy, cost, maintenance, and longevity in order to provide energy "servants." More simple, long-lasting technology with fewer conveniences (that often turn out to be maintenance *inconveniences*), permit a given family income to go farther and, therefore, create an increase in usable income and in many ways a "higher" standard of living.

We have over the years continuously added technological complexity, under the assumption that perpetual growth in production and income could perpetually support increased complexity and increased numbers of technological possessions. Now, in this new era of slow growth and increasingly high energy costs, we must make changes in technology, lifestyle, and what we formerly meant by "standard of living."

Automatic transmissions on cars are part of the old era. Simple manual transmissions are longer lasting and cheaper to make, provide more control of the car, and in most cases are more energy efficient. A plan by the automobile industry to convert Americans to automatic transmissions has been very effective during the last quarter century, beginning with driver education in schools which taught young people to use automatic transmissions. The sexist stereotype was exploited to get women to expect automatic transmissions, as though they were not bright enough to learn to use a manual transmission. In fact, the skill can be acquired in a matter of minutes, but millions of women are still locked into the belief, accepted by their husbands, that the family car must have an automatic transmission. The new liberation movement needs to include, in its large agenda, women's liberation from costly, energy-consuming, obsolete technology.

Homes can be built at lower cost, be accessible to more people, and require less maintenance without dishwashers, disposals, two-oven stoves, swimming pools and saunas. Life without these items may be worse for some people, better for others. They are minor conveniences at significant economic and energy costs, and they should be added only to suit the special needs of a family, rather than as a standard package for homes and apartments. In a resource-limited world, it is possible either for many people to live under adequate but modest conditions, or for a few to live in opulent waste while the majority live in poverty. High-energy/high-resource consumption is not only unnecessary for a good life but dangerous to the social and political fabric of the modern world. Yet in our energy future, we do not need to turn the clock back to the early part of the twentieth century, when people used much less of the conventional forms of energy. The twenty-first century can have energy use levels similar to the present level, if populations do not increase drastically. The various forms of renewable, incoming solar energy are the key to life in the twenty-first century. Our energy planning should treat fossil fuels as transitional fuels, giving way to solar energy on a schedule geared to their abundance. Petroleum is the *least* abundant of the fossil fuels, gas is next, and coal follows.

Thermodynamics

The first "law" of thermodynamics which is learned by students of physics is that energy is not increased or decreased but only transformed. The total amount of energy is always the same. Heat may change into chemical energy through photosynthesis or the burning of gasoline may produce heat transmitted into the air. This law applies to the total universe, and while it is of value to astronomers, it has little practical value here on earth.

The second law applies to human life and is known as the entropy law. Its principle is just the opposite of the first law, that *available* energy always *decreases* during transformation or use. Energy systems go downhill. The sun is slowly burning out. When electricity is used to turn a motor, inefficiency is inevitable. The motor will not do as much work as the energy put into it. The loss is in heat energy. When sunlight is captured by plants, only a small percentage of the energy is converted to use by the plant.

We therefore cannot avoid energy inefficiency. But what we can do is to minimize inefficiency and move toward the use of the incoming, renewable energy of the sun. Our future is then tied to the decay rate of the sun, which is exceedingly low. An estimated five billion years remain.

Matching the kind of energy needed with the right use is basic to energy conservation. Consider the process of burning natural gas to run a generator to produce electricity to heat water: There is considerable energy loss in the burning of the gas to create the electricity, and then more loss as the electricity is used to heat a wire in order to heat the water. We can eliminate these wasteful intermediate steps and heat much more water directly with gas water heaters.

Electricity should be connected to high-efficiency uses such as turning electric motors. Electricity is a "high quality" form of energy requiring other forms of energy to produce alternate current and controlled voltage. If you only need heat for manufacturing, the burning of combustible material will usually produce the highest efficiency. Though a very high welding temperature might require *electric* welding, a lower welding temperature can use hydrogen and oxygen.

Nuclear power plants exemplify waste and mismatching when their electricity is used to produce heat. The exceedingly high temperatures of reactors are used to *boil water* at 212°F. The boiling water produces steam to run an electric generator. The heat waste is so enormous that either the top of the generator is a huge wide stack which discharges a constant plume of steam, or else a large body of water is required to absorb the excess heat—which is simply wasted. If the electricity is producing heat, the efficiency is very low compared to bypassing nuclear power and heating directly with natural gas, bio-gas, or direct solar energy.

Our habits of building energy inefficiency into our economy arose in an era of seeming abundance, when energy waste became part of the way of life. Now we need energy planning that matches energy use and energy quality.

The principle of entropy applies to geology and ecology. Minerals were condensed in many places on earth. Little energy is required to obtain condensed deposits, but once that mineral is dispersed to dumps, air, and water, it requires much more energy to recover it again. We reduce energy consumption by preventing the dispersion of minerals: Reusing them through recycling reduces entropy.

The same concept applies to topsoil, crucial to the plants that generate oxygen and provide wood, watershed control, and food. Mismanagement of plants and forests results in topsoil depletion. Topsoil uses solar energy to store plant nutrients. Its replacement requires enormous amounts of energy to generate synthetic nutrients. Topsoil is part of our life-sustaining heritage generated over millions of years, yet topsoil loss in the United States is increasing and is even greater now than during the dust bowl years of the thirties. Clearcutting of forests on steep slopes, breaking of surface vegetation such as grasses, and lowering of water tables that feed vegetation are practices that displace topsoil from the land, sending it into the streams to destroy spawning grounds of fish and into ocean estuaries to kill the breeding grounds of sea life. The 1977 United Nations conference on Desertification reported that about one-fifth of the world's cropland has been degraded and is headed toward worldwide destruction of life sustaining vegetation.[6]

Thermodynamic principles are crucial to our future, requiring matching of kinds of energy, reducing the energy loss from its source, and working within a sustainable energy source that does not degrade the basic ecosystem. For instance, to put heat into the earth's atmosphere from nuclear power or fossil fuels based on ancient solar energy involves the thermal pollution of the biosphere. The balance between incoming solar energy and what is leaving the earth is changed. The resulting increase in the earth's temperature can change weather, plants, insects, animals, and the ecological life support system. It also affects rain, the source of hydroelectric energy. Our energy future then becomes uncertain, more likely degraded than improved. The human implications are starvation, disease, reductions of standards of living, and the social conflicts that are likely to be caused by a decline in the quality of life and the survival base of the planet.

PROPOSED ENERGY STRATEGIES

Energy proposals generated in the 1970s and 1980s were based on the following four models:

1. Find more conventional energy and continue with present lifestyles and economic goals.

2. Focus on conservation of conventional sources and move toward solar energy. Do not change basic lifestyles or economic goals.

3. Focus on conservation of conventional sources, move toward solar energy, and also move toward a decentralized, market-based society.

4. Focus on conservation of conventional sources during transition and shift to incoming solar energy. Achieve transition through integrated planning of jobs, transportation, housing, agriculture, and a different form of national defense. Let us examine each of these in turn.

1. More-of-the-same (the Reagan administration approach)

More-of-the-same involves continued reliance on petroleum, increased use of coal and gas, increased use of nuclear power, and increased use of hydroelectric power. This means increasing production and supply of conventional energy sources. The Carter administration made use of some energy price controls; the Reagan administration has emphasized decontrol. Carter stressed conversion of shale and coal into synthetic fuels and the reduction of waste, but Reagan has not supported synthetic fuel development, or encouraged reduction in waste, only an increase in supply of fossil fuels and nuclear power.

This model presumes a continually expanded GNP based on energy supply growth, and requires military might in the Near East to insure control over our oil-based future. It relies on strong profit incentives for large corporations and presumes that highly centralized and expensive plants and industries will supply energy through complex grids and industrial outlets. Profit-making incentive is presumed to constitute the economic basis for overcoming shortage by "opening up" public lands, the oceans, and exploring more deeply and in more places.

Model 1: Evaluation

The best way to evaluate models is on the basis of likely consequences. The first model, more-of-the-same, continues to concentrate on the supply of energy through nonrenewable sources—oil, gas, coal, and nuclear energy. Large-scale, concentrated, capital intensive industries are to deliver energy using both market incentive and public subsidy.

Since oil and gas constitute a short-term prospect, this model is forced to rely on coal and nuclear. From nuclear fuel one can make only electricity, which is the least needed form of energy. Furthermore, nuclear is the most dangerous of energy technologies. Its plants and fuel sources are short-lived, disposal of wastes remains an unsolved problem, social disruptions are high, and, finally, nuclear energy is not competitive. So coal is the key to the future under this model.

Though coal is nonrenewable, it is sufficiently abundant to last between 200 and 400 years, depending on demand. But the mining of coal is destructive to the land and produces pollution; and underground mining is a serious threat to the health of workers.

Coal can be converted to gas and to a liquid fuel. This is a feasible technology, currently in use in some parts of the world, but the conversion and the use of the fuel in any form is highly polluting. One serious consequence of the increased industrial use of coal is the production of acid rain. The lower the grade of coal, the more pollution—lung polluting sulfuric acids and unpleasant smells.

This model for our energy future tries to keep intact the old industrial economy with its centralized corporate power. It ignores the current decline in heavy industry as we move toward an information-service economy. It ignores the price paid for public external costs of a high-polluting economy in health and quality of life. It does not even take account of the exponentially increasing energy costs that come from high capital intensive energy sources, which could make people slaves *to* energy instead of masters of energy.

This model, clearly supported by the Reagan administration, ignores planning that serves human employment and quality of life, and therefore chooses an energy future using industries that employ the least numbers of people but provide the most profits for corporations. A country so dependent on centralized technology and corporate power is vulnerable to capitalist exploitation of citizens with less power, especially the poor and the minorities. In addition, as the Lovins have made so clear in *Brittle Power*, any large centralized power facility—nuclear, oil, coal—makes a country weak and vulnerable to terrorism.

A country still operating on petroleum and converting to coal would be desperately dependent on short-term petroleum and would require a large military force in areas such as the Near East, ready to take over foreign oil fields if necessary, provoking World War III. (The threat of this strategy, which was developed under the Carter administration, continues under the Reagan adminstration.)

This first model, therefore, portends a future of international neo-fascist political power, maintained to obtain scarce fuel by force if necessary. Such a future would also unavoidably feature an arms race to protect an increasingly vulnerable old-style economy.

In addition to increasing the dangers of war and internal violence, this model cannot take us very far into the future. Knowing that transition is merely delayed can have a profoundly depressing effect on a population, especially upon youth, who would have reason to think adults were escaping the responsibility of facing up to hard decisions by handing them over to their children. A deep and destructive pessimism is likely to engulf a society that fails to deal with the realities of fossil fuel scarcity and the necessity of transition to a sustainable future.

2. The conservation-with-conventional-economics model
(The Ford Foundation and Harvard Model: A Time to Choose, 1974,[7] and Energy Future, 1979 [8])

The conservation-with-conventional-economics model proposes the use of government planning to achieve modest reduction in energy consumption so that instead of increasing consumption, zero energy growth would occur. Most of the changes would come through technical fixes, more fuel-efficient automobiles, and better efficiency in heating and cooling. Regulation, tax incentives, and selective deregulation of prices would be used.

Much of the rest of the economy would remain the same, but in the Harvard model there would be special emphasis on the elimination of waste. Energy conserved is equal to new energy supplies; it costs much less to save and the saved energy becomes rapidly available for other uses.

These two studies helped to break the traditional idea that economic growth relies directly on energy *supply*. By emphasizing technological changes that would provide greater efficiency, we can reduce energy waste. This moderate position suggested little need for changing the United States' economic system and lifestyle. It was a foot in the door, however, opening up the possibility of conservation planning in both the public and private sectors, and it came from middle-of-the-road, establishment sources. Private corporations, especially the oil industries, found its deregulation proposals to be attractive, and conservationists liked the waste reduction, energy efficiency, and recognition of limits to nonrenewable resources.

The Harvard study states, "Even with price controls, U.S. domestic oil production will fall substantially by 1990, perhaps by three to four million barrels per day."[9] Dependence on imported oil was seen as a threat to peace, encouraging a large military establishment to insure access to foreign oil and placing small nations in an economic squeeze in which they compete with the United States for their oil purchases.

Oil will rise in price, according to the Harvard model, so that conversion to other fuels and conversion to greater efficiency and less waste will take place largely without government aid. But some aid is advocated and the Harvard report proposes tax breaks and revisions of building codes to accommodate solar energy construction, because solar energy has less of a constituency and less basis for capital formation.

Conservation and use of solar energy are considered the cheapest and most rapid ways to have more usable energy, but both require assistance through government planning, according to the Ford and Harvard reports.

Model 2: Evaluation

There is merit in these proposals insofar as they come to terms with scarcity, the end of the petroleum era, and the potentiality of solar energy. They accept the need for public-federal energy policy. They appeal to a broad political spectrum, for they encourage price decontrol on oil and gas and elimination of subsidy such as the depletion allowance on oil. To do this, however, they make excessive concessions to the petroleum industry, including condoning hazardous solutions (offshore oil drilling). They support short-range nuclear energy so that *total* energy is maximized. But they fail to point out that the electricity supplied by nuclear is not the kind of energy most needed. Heat energy is in short supply. Some areas such as the Pacific Northwest have surplus electricity.

Their proposals for reducing waste by making oil more expensive, stopping heat waste in buildings, cutting down on fuel-wasting transportation, and lowering energy use in manufacturing (following the Europeans) are clearly necessary, though insufficient. Tax rewards and punishments and such bold proposals as subsidizing free public transportation (Harvard) are attempts to plan transition and redress equity for the impact of high-cost oil through the use of government power.

This call for major change in the economy raises the question of whether a government that has so long been a captive of the economic wealth of large corporations can really plan for the public interest by tinkering a bit with the economy. The conflict between transition planning in the public interest and the short-run planning of big corporations to serve their own economic interests makes all public sector planning in the United States a precarious undertaking. The odds for successful public planning would be higher if *economic and environmental changes were coupled with changes in political power.*

The Ford-Harvard studies may ask for too *little* change and run into the same problems in social change that exist in ecological change—namely, "we cannot do merely one thing." If jobs, transportation, education, the control of production ownership, political power, and political structures are highly interrelated and organic, the Ford-Harvard proposals, by asking for half a loaf, may get virtually nothing at all. This is a difficult and conjectural question, however, for it is also possible that if these proposals begin to put even small changes into effect, they may produce conditions by which bolder transition planning can later occur—or, because of their inadequacy, they may open the door for backlash. Ford and Harvard are in the genus of short-range incremental plans, acting in the hope that next stages will be planned at a later time so that the full transition will eventually be achieved.

Neither of these plans offers a sufficient basis for a twenty-first century energy future. Too many private sector forces are left intact. Some of these are competitive market forces, many are giant corporate monopolies; all are giving separate, fragmented attention to their own self-interest.

Considering that these proposals come from Ford and the Harvard Business School ethos, they are bold energy proposals, useful achievements for the 1970s when waste was acceptable and conservation was not. Their naivete about the use of political power may explain, however, how the Reagan administration was able to proceed as though these proposals did not exist. They do not address fundamental questions of a long-run sustainable economy providing employment and based on energy-carrying capacity. They separate energy policy from resources policy and fail to confront such imperative questions as transition from the nuclear war system, which must be a major consideration in transition planning. This failure to put energy transition within an integrated transition plan is a fatal flaw in these proposals, probably stemming from excessive faith in the ability of the forces of market supply and demand to bring about a better future.

3. The Conservation-with-Decentralization model (The Amory Lovins Model: Soft Energy Paths, 1977)[10]

Lovins' *Conservation with Decentralization* model is a logical alternative to the Ford-Harvard proposals.[7] It assumes that we should keep government *away* from energy transition and base the transition on economic costs. Changes in the last few years, especially with the decline of expensive nuclear power, have been consistent with Lovins' prediction. Ideologically, he has strong support from libertarian conservatives, community-oriented radicals, and conservation organizations such as Friends of the Earth.

His evidence that bigness is usually energy *inefficient* shows how often big business such as oil, gas, nuclear, and coal is subsidized. Therefore, a truly open competitive market will reward smallness. Then small is not only "beautiful" but also economic, and if economics is the central force for change, the current centralized system of corporate capitalism will wither away into decentralization and community control without violent revolution. The United States will then be a modern version of the Jeffersonian version of the good society.

Since our waste-making, over-consuming society is tied to large-scale, capital intensive nonrenewable forms of energy which control the lives of Americans and extract unnecessary profit from them, the shift to renewable forms of solar energy will be a shift toward less economic exploitation and toward giving people greater control over their lives. Solar energy is distributed by the sun rather than by Big Oil and it can be captured with less capital by those who use it. The fossil fuel world is tied to resources ownership and depletion allowances; whereas, use of solar energy decentralizes energy sources and produces a nonviolent revolution in energy access.

Lovins' believes government planning is so tied to big corporations that he rejects social planning through government. The open market will be the distributor; good values will presumably result for the society as a whole without explicit social goals. Narrow self-interest motives will produce good public results from the "unseen hand" of the market. Economics then shifts from being the dismal science to being a benevolent god with gifts from the sun.

According to this model, nuclear energy, coal, and petroleum will yield to methane, alcohol, photovoltaics, and active and passive forms of solar architecture. Nonsolar energy will phase itself out as its scarcity produces higher prices. Technological efficiency will be encouraged to assist efficiency of nonrenewables and to permit use of solar-based renewables because solar forms of energy will increasingly cost less.

Lovins presumes there should be no public policy attempt to change people's values but expects the combination of cost and self-interest to produce changes in values and lifestyle. He has faith that people will choose smaller cars, will ride bicycles, and will travel less, for example. Industry will decentralize as the energy-cost inefficiencies of large industry make the changes necessary.

Lovins' assumptions project a predominantly solar-based economy in the twenty-first century, relying on least cost competition. In addition, this transition to solar-based energy will, according to Lovins, lessen the dangers of war by moving away from nuclear power with its plutonium by-products feeding into nuclear bombs and terrorist weapons. By decoupling from petroleum, the United States would have less reason to connect national security with protection of the Near East oil fields, thereby making Soviet-American war less likely and lessening the need for a large military system to protect the Near East.

Model 3: Evaluation

The deficiency of this model is based mainly on its lack of examination of what the open market does compared to what people can do if they are involved in explicit social planning. Lovins cannot advocate an open market only for energy. His nonplanning ideology would apply to other areas too.

Even though high energy prices might have good energy conservation results, a society without public planning would have extremes in income distribution, no controls over pollution, and no rights to employment. Among the inequities the Lovins plan fosters would be a preference for the rural citizen over the city resident, for self-sufficiency is more feasible in rural areas that can create their own methane and burn wood for fuel without severe pollution effects.

Movement toward solar-based energy would reduce pollution, but without government controls and planning the fossil burners of the next score of decades during transition would have the public pay for the costs of their pollution, since prohibitions would have to be controlled by government. Similarly, the dumping of toxic wastes in a market economy without tight public controls would produce the disasters that are currently apparent. In a market system pollution pays—for the polluter.

Transition from the war system requires the most widespread planning, on a planetary level. Lovins' decentralization would keep power in the hands of multinationals and nations, and the war system could lead to nuclear war, even though national energy self-sufficiency might help defuse specific crisis areas such as the Near East.

Lovins' model has considerable appeal to Americans who nurture romantic images of the past, with a simple life unencumbered by the complications of public planning. But the unemployed will support job security before supporting solar energy, whether it is cost effective or not. And the Third World will not expect the political power of corporate capitalism to wither away as energy technology changes. Those who suffer from pollution from air or water, as in Love Canal, will not accept a society that has no public policies guaranteeing people a right to a healthful environment.

Lovins' nonplanning world is not even possible, for the real question is not whether there is to be planning. Rather, it is who will plan and for what purposes? Lovins is right that planning is now largely in the hands of the Pentagon and large corporations, but planning can either continue to be mainly in the service of special interests or can be directed increasingly toward public interests.

Lovins' decentralization ideology avoids analysis to determine the appropriate level of response to a planning goal. Some environmental issues require global levels of response—ocean pollution, ocean resources, atmospheric testing of nuclear weapons. Disposal of toxic waste requires at least a national level of planning. Medical and employment rights must be national. Lovins' excessive localism would contribute to political and social fragmentation rather than to a widening structure of law and justice. His *laissez-faire* economics undermines his admirable objective of a benign and sustainable energy source. The means conflict with the goals.

Another way to understand Lovins' position is to compare it with Barry Commoner's. Both of them are very astute in analyzing technical elements of natural systems, energy production, and economic costs. But then they part company. Lovins believes political planning is unnecessary.

Similarities and differences can be illustrated in their mutual interest in converting solar energy to alcohol to produce what is called ethanol for fueling internal combustion engines. Both Lovins and Commoner have analyzed the question of technical feasibility and agree that there are no major obstacles. Both agree that ethanol reduces pollution, requiring no toxic chemicals such as tetraethyl lead or other additives. Pure ethanol has an octane rating of 118, permitting higher compression without spark knock. Both agree that political power of automobile and oil companies has been used to deter use of ethanol. Both agree that a serious social question, the use of land to produce fuel, is a matter that can be solved without reducing food production. There are other sources of ethanol such as garbage and wood fiber from paper, sawdust, and forestry waste. Plants can be grown and processed to provide ethanol and high-grade animal food at the same time. There is surplus farm production in the United States and most of the food that is grown is fed to animals. Dietary change of food low on the food chain could aid the solution.

But after agreement on technical feasibility and social desirability, we find Lovins advocating prices in a *laissez-faire* market system as the means for effecting transition. Commoner, however, says that regulation of agriculture under the New Deal and under recent administrations has prevented transition to ethanol by getting farmers to plow crops under and produce less. "Government failed to solve the problem of agricultural overproduction not because it regulated agriculture but because its regulations were misdirected. If government instead were to facilitate the introduction of a crop system capable of producing ethanol as well as food and suitably integrated with the necessary changes in the oil and automobile industries, farmers would be better off, and the nation would be on the way to a more stable, solar economy."[11]

The decentralization that Lovins proposes as the way to curb the power of Big Oil is not feasible in urbanized areas where city dwellers cannot produce much ethanol on their own property. Big Oil can, however, be restrained through integrated democratic planning of the economy because political power in a democracy has the potential to override corporate power. This position is the one supported in this book and described in the following fourth alternative.

4. The Conservation Through Integrated Planning model (proposed in this book)

In this plan energy change is not the only goal. The plan treats energy sustainability as only one aspect of resource sustainability and uses the most integrated planning of the four models to serve a number of goals: common quality of life, resource sustainability, carrying capacity, employment, national security, economic fairness, human development, and the rights of future generations. These values are integrated into planning goals to guide public policy and public administration. Planning is local, regional, statewide, national, international and/or global according to the problem being considered. Since economic planning, resource planning, and environmental quality planning require national policy, the planning framework must be mainly national. Because the current energy base uses resources that are not sustainable and are highly polluting, and because the centralized and highly capitalized industries that provide these resources are relatively low job producers, transition to a sustainable *incoming* energy base is an important part of this form of planning.

Waste of nonrenewable resources becomes a way of "stealing" our common heritage and denying rights of future generations. We must have energy efficiency and resource recycling to provide production which serves human needs within a sustainable carrying capacity.

The private sector would be regulated to serve the *public* interest with human needs instead of human wants being first priority goals. This would be done with positive incentives where possible (taxes, land use, education, and public encouragement) but with restrictions and penalties where necessary. Serious violations become criminal acts so that people who willfully destroy nonrenewable resources or threaten our life-support system become liable to prosecution.

Statutory and constitutional laws at county, state, and federal levels would specify the goals and the means to achieve them. Government should be strong enough to achieve the goals, but the private sector should be allowed to flourish within the framework of public goals. A clear set of national policies are needed to control economic growth, economic distribution, and to realize human rights. Long-range goals, more predictability of monetary policy, greater job opportunity, and resources that are recycled and sustainable would be used to add significantly to the real productivity and efficiency of the economic system, now subject to wasteful booms and depressions as well as piecemeal, short-range, and often contradictory efforts at remedies. Energy is currently squandered and wasted when it is profitable to do so. This model would constrain profitability within an integrated planning system that connects short- and long-range public interest goals providing transition lead time. Under the old system, capital gains and mineral depletion have been subsidized through preferential taxes; this model would use depletion *taxes* instead of *subsidies* to serve the new goals and capital gains would be taxed as ordinary income. Integrated, long-range national goals would tie in a number of simultaneous considerations to guide and control change toward a future chosen by the public through debate and election. Alternative feasible models, each with various integrated patterns of trade-offs, would provide the basis for selecting the preferred alternative as a set of policy goals for the United States. Each model would need to include transition steps from the war system and the military-industrial complex to world law and a peace economy. Each feasible model would guarantee employment within a sustainable energy-based economy, and economic priorities would focus on the most urgent human needs. Such a framework would permit states and localities to fit in according to their special differences.

This way of planning for energy use puts energy into the service of human needs, and it uses political power which is democratic and public to control the economic system. All three previously analyzed energy models retain such a large amount of private sector economic power that private wealth and corporate power become the determiners of our energy future and of the quality of our lives.

Our energy problems were not caused only by accidents of history. Corporate giants in the "private" sector have engaged in very effective planning to *serve their purposes.* Henry Ford in the 1930s engaged in a struggle to use agricultural ethanol as a motor fuel but the more powerful oil industry was effective in keeping American transportation on the petroleum path.[12]

During that same period, people throughout the United States rode in effective electric city street cars for 5¢ and often did not need to buy an automobile. Then General Motors, Standard Oil of California, and Firestone joined together to buy up trolley lines and replace them with petroleum burning buses, which provided profits to all three companies. By 1949 one hundred electric trolley systems, including Los Angeles', were replaced with GM buses. There was little smog in Los Angeles prior to that time.

The three companies were convicted in 1949 of criminal conspiracy in a Chicago federal court. General Motors was fined $5,000 and their treasurer who aided in dismantling of the Los Angeles trolley system was fined $1.[13]

By contrast, most European governments during this same period were creating the world's best system of fast, efficient, low-cost rail travel that was later rivaled by the Japanese.

Some current trends in the United States are already contributing to the transition. Heavy industry has been the largest energy consumer, but there has been a decline in heavy industries such as steel and aluminum and an increase in service and information industries. In addition, most recent commercial and residential construction has helped reduce energy consumption. High heating costs, revised building codes, and economic incentives provided by utilities have been the main prompters of the change.

Automobile fuels are not limited to petroleum. Coal can be liquified as it was in Germany in World War II and is currently done in South Africa. Alcohol (gasohol) is already in occasional use in the United States and is common in Brazil. Hydrogen can be used in cars.

But other trends, traffic congestion and economic costs that increase faster than per capita income, make the automobile less and less useful. The automobile of the twenty-first century will need to be much more fuel efficient and much less dominant as transportation. Today's widespread use of large gas-guzzling automobiles to transport only one or two people will not be tolerable. They currently waste precious petroleum, depriving people in the future who could use it efficiently.

Car rental will increasingly make sense for occasional vacations, especially if a family needs a larger car only for periodic travel. People could also own a piece of annual automobile time as they now cooperatively own part of a time-shared condominium.

Cities can become much more desirable without automobiles in the inner core. Bicycles, mass transit, small, slow quiet mini-vehicles, and more walking in an automobile-free environment could help make inner cities attractive places. The automobile is the destroyer of cities. It pollutes air, causes congestion, is involved in pedestrian injuries, makes noise, and consumes land and parking space at such an astronomical price that its total cost prevents payment for many necessary social needs.

We need to create a future that can be sustained and does not steal energy and resources from future generations. Such planning is only one facet of the cluster of objectives needed to have a safer, more just future, and a more interesting way of life.

Energy is only one kind of resource. All resources are part of the environment that sustains life. The kind of integrated planning that connects energy and responsible human values will be developed in more detail in the next two chapters, which examine economics and public planning. The main energy transition requirements are illustrated by an outline that shows what needs to be decreased and what needs to be increased.

From Nonrenewable Energy to Renewable Energy

1. The Technical Dimension

(Less)	(More)
Transportation by automobile, airplane, and truck	Transportation by boat, train, bus, motorbike, bicycle, and walking
Fuel from gasoline, diesel, and gas	Fuel from alcohol, methane, wood, solar heat (passive and active). Temporary use of coal

(Less)	(More)
Electricity from nuclear, oil, gas, coal	Electricity from photovoltaic, hydroelectric, ocean thermal conversion
Heat-wasting architecture	Highly insulated construction with retrofit
Emphasis on energy generation	Emphasis on energy conservation

2. The Political Dimension—Public Planning

(Less)	(More)
Corporate and Pentagon planning of the future	Public planning with integrated goals, long-range transition to a sustainable energy base
High capital intensive, low employment, high waste, petroleum-based economy	Skilled services, economic priorities, goods related to a sustainable energy base
Multinational industries supported globally by national military forces	Global planning of peacekeeping economic goals, and sustainable resources
Petroleum-based agriculture	Renewable resource-based agriculture
Taxes encouraging large cars and transcontinental meetings	Taxes discouraging large cars and transcontinental meetings
Subsidy of truck and car highways	Subsidy to trains, buses, and low-cost mass transit
Nonrenewable resource subsidy	Nonrenewable resource tax
Renewable resource subsidy

NOTES

1. Carroll L. Wilson, Director, *Energy: Global Prospects 1985–2000* (New York: McGraw-Hill, 1977), pp. 111–46.

2. Ibid, pp. 3–4.

3. Amory Lovins and Hunter Lovins, *Energy and War: Breaking the Nuclear Link* (San Francisco: Friends of the Earth, 1981).

4. Also see Pat Choate, et al., *America in Ruins* (Durham, NC: Duke Univ. Press Policy Studies, 1983).

5. Lester R. Brown, et al., *Running on Empty: The Future of the Automobile in an Oil Short World*, (New York: W. W. Norton, 1979).

6. Erik P. Eckholm, *Losing Ground* (New York: W. W. Norton, 1976).

7. S. David Freeman, Director, *A Time to Choose* (Cambridge, MA: Ballinger Publishing Co., 1974).

8. Robert Stobaugh and Daniel Yergin, eds., *Energy Future* (New York: Ballantine Books, 1980).

9. Ibid., p. 301.

10. Amory Lovins, *Soft Energy Paths: Toward a Durable Peace* (Cambridge, MA: Ballinger, 1977).

11. Barry Commoner, "A Reporter at Large (Ethanol)," *New Yorker* (October 10, 1983), p. 153.

12. Ibid., pp. 151–52.

13. This case is well known in legal literature. For a summary, see Barry Commoner, *The Poverty of Power* (New York: Bantam, 1976) pp. 177–79.

SELECTED READINGS

Barbour, Ian G. 1980. *Technology, Environment, and Human Values.* New York: Praeger.

Brown, Lester. Christopher Flavin, and Colin Norman. 1979. *The Future of the Automobile in an Oil-Short World.* Washington, DC: Worldwatch, Paper 32.

Ehrlich, Paul, Anne Ehrlich, and John Holdren. 1977. *Ecoscience: Population, Resources, Environment.* San Francisco: W. H. Freeman.

Green, Maurice B. 1977. *Eating Oil: Energy Use in Food Production.* Boulder, Colorado; Westview Press.

Hammond, Allen, William Metz, and Thomas Maugh III. 1973. *Energy and the Future.* Washington, DC: American Association for the Advancement of Science.

Hayes, Denis. 1978. *Repairs, Reuse, Recycling—First Steps Toward a Sustainable Society.* Washington DC: Worldwatch, Paper 23, Worldwatch Institute.

Meadows, Dennis L. 1977. *Alternatives to Growth I.* Cambridge, MA: Ballinger.

Nash, Hugh, ed. 1979. *The Energy Controversy: Soft Path Questions and Answers.* San Francisco: Friends of the Earth.

National Geographic, *Energy: Special Report.* 1981. Washington, DC: National Geographic.

Norman, Colin. 1978. *Soft Technologies, Hard Choices.* Washington, DC: Worldwatch, Paper 21.

Ophuls, William. 1977. *Ecology and the Politics of Scarcity.* San Francisco: W. H. Freeman.

Pirages, Dennis. 1977. *The Sustainable Society.* New York: Praeger.

4

21st Century
Economics

If Americans in the twenty-first century have a better understanding of the different forms of economics, they will probably be amazed at the primitive level of economic thought held by the public and by decision makers today. The current "opiate of the masses" is in the area of economics; American economic thought and practices are probably the most primitive and anachronistic in the industrial world.

Economics is concerned with the production and distribution of goods and services. The numbers of people employed, what they produce, who receives the production — these are dependent on the political policies of government and the goals of the people who participate in the economy. The only real limits are in the finite resources of nature and the state of technology. Yet the United States has over 12 million people involuntarily unemployed, most goods are overproduced, air, water, and land are polluted and increasingly depleted, the distribution of both goods and services is unfair, and the power of unequal wealth corrupts government in the United States and throughout the world. We use U.S. military power to support the American form of economics and we do so in the name of "freedom."

Economics is viewed by the majority of Americans as a set of laws that operate outside of human control. Our central economic "planning" activity continues to be the prediction of trends in order to adjust individual and corporate behavior in anticipation of them. Clearly this is the way the stock market game is played. Real estate values, interest rates, employment levels, inflation, and all areas of economic concern are built on the belief in trends, and those who gaze either into crystal balls or computers to guide investors and buyers do so in reliance upon this conventional wisdom.

Whether such conventional wisdom is wise or foolish is of fundamental importance. Are there better alternatives, where trends are not merely anticipated but largely controlled to serve people? Can the social laws that apply to economics be distinguished from laws of nature that apply to biology, chemistry, and physics? If Americans obey the "law" of supply and demand are they obeying *reality* as they do when they "obey" the law of gravity? Or, do they abdicate choice over economic policy and commit one of the great ironies of history—supporting a form of slavery while claiming to support freedom?

But the current alternatives are not as clear cut as they were in the early thirties when government intervention produced a mixed economy in response to the crisis of the Great Depression. *Laissez-faire* (neo-classical) economics have been modified with a Keynesian application of fiscal and monetary control by government and infusion of funds through social programs, retirement benefits, the building of roads and schools, and medical subsidies. This "liberal" epoch was challenged by the Reagan administration, and an updated version of predepression classical economics of the 1920s has been reinstated. The rest of the world was amazed and shocked to find that the old mystique was sufficiently alive and well enough to secure a plurality constituency. Within two years after the 1980 presidential election, this retrograde economics had produced the largest depression since the '30s, causing record rates of unemployment, bankruptcy, economic maldistribution, and federal deficits. The major difference from the 1920s was that Reagan embarked on a massive escalation in the arms race, both conventional and nuclear. The twenties were, by comparison, militarily benign.

The national elections of '82 returned the same number of senators back to Washington to support Reaganomics, though 26 Reaganomics supporters in the House were voted out. Democrats wanted to tilt spending somewhat more toward social programs and to increase military spending at a slightly lower rate than Republicans. There was more rising disillusionment with Reaganomics than with President Reagan. Presumably he was not accountable for mismanagement of the economy because management of the economy had not yet been accepted as a responsibility of government or the President. Moreover, economic management was presumed to be only a matter of tinkering a bit with the laws of supply and demand. Reagan claimed his plan was to shift the control of the American future more to the private sector and the "market" by shrinking government and expanding the power of corporations and small business. He called for more than doubling the military budget in five years, producing high interest rates. And, he granted tax cuts to corporations and those in high income brackets. The fact that most small businesses have contracted rather than expanded and that many corporations have shrunk or were liquidated due to the economic recession did not sway Reagan or the supporters of Reaganomics, for in their minds there were only two perceived alternatives—an inflation producing, Democratic, big government economy, or an economy run by corporate business for the enhancement of corporate income.

How could *laissez-faire* economics, rugged indivdualism, and the early view that "the best government is the least government" persist for so long in the United States? For various reasons economic thought in the United States is both relatively narrow and unimaginative. American culture developed in an historical context in which people who wished to escape the tyranny of centralized European governments came to a vast resource-rich land seeking economic advantages by becoming homesteaders, pioneers, and exploiters of what seemed to be unlimited resources. The "freedom" to exploit these resources became a national religion. Fertile farmland, vast forests, open ranges, coal, hydro-power, and abundant petroleum provided more opportunity for each person to gain material abundance through hard work and initiative than people had ever experienced before.

Though the context has changed, much of the old outlook persists. Former abundance has been depleted — oil, iron ore, copper, forests, topsoil. Most rivers are dammed. The new entrepreneurs are huge multinational corporations that invest in developing societies which provide the lowest labor and materials costs and the highest profits. Individual employment is typically dependent more on the economic policies of corporations and government than on personal initiative. Rugged individualism gives way to frustration and insecurity as people become pawns in an economic game over which they have little or no sense of control. Surprisingly, the underlying theory of Reaganomics is that the best economy is actually one that is *out of control*. If the logic escapes you, here it is again: Control is tyranny, being out of control is freedom. An economy that is out of control is a "free" economy.

Little wonder that people who are bewildered, lost, frustrated, and insecure economically search for scapegoats to blame for our national difficulties. The unemployed victims of these cruel policies are mainly minorities and women who are often viewed as the *cause* of the problem, a phenomenon called "blame the victim." To the extent that people do not understand that each form of economics is an invented social game with rules that determine outcomes, they presume that the economic effects on individuals were *caused* by those individuals. When people lack understanding of economics as a *system*, they often use the old metaphysics of individualism to support the belief that (1) each person has free will and can choose his destiny, and (2) if someone is unemployed he has chosen to be and can choose to work if he wishes. Therefore, unemployment is not a social problem, it is an individual problem. Since it is individual, it does not require a *political* solution.

What, in fact, characterizes the modern world is the use of political power to produce social effects. Before the twentieth century, political power was used to extract taxes, to wage war with nations, to suppress threats to established government, and to extract wealth from colonies through coercion. Modern governments have added the function of using political power to organize and plan the economy. Political power can be used in two ways: (1) positively, to produce desired goals, or (2) negatively, to shift power to other areas of the society. Reaganomics is based mainly on the negative use of governmental power, the attempt to liquidate as much governmental power and responsibility as possible so that it will be used to serve the goals of the private sector. But the private sector is a planning system, an economy based on corporate capitalism where corporations exercise primary control over the economy, e.g., as in decontrol of natural gas prices. Instead of an economy serving public interests, it primarily serves private profit—and we move from political democracy to corporate oligarchy.[1]

Such an ideology requires public acceptance. Political propaganda and its salesmen must persuade the public to give away their political power and to believe that private profit equals the public interest—that if Exxon, ITT, U.S. Steel, GM, and other corporations fluorish, the interests of the American public are being served.

Reaganomics de-democratizes. It tries to liquidate whatever system exists for providing public participation in the determination of economic policy. It shifts power to the private sector and ensures that government does *not* work well. Secretary of the Interior Watt, EPA Director Anne (Gorsuch) Burford, Secretary of Energy Edwards, and Secretary of Education Bell tried to cripple government agencies when they could not stifle their functions. They also centered public criticism of themselves rather than on Reagan, to keep the image of a well-intentioned President separated from the agencies and policies for which the President is responsible.

Under Reaganomics everyone is to be responsible except the President. The unemployed are encouraged to blame themselves and "vote with their feet" as Reagan calls it, by going somewhere else to get a job. But, if it becomes clear that too few jobs are available, the President is still not to be blamed, for "laws" of supply and demand which transcend presidential power are then the cause. If there is a downturn in the economy, business "cycles" will require, by definition, an upturn. So we should be patient, "stay the course," and avoid placing any responsibility on the governing administration, including the President himself. Rather, the political propaganda of Reaganomics tries to place the blame on the individual citizen.

This set of circumstances can continue as long as people believe that natural laws of supply and demand rather than political power govern economics, that government is largely without value and should not be involved in social planning and that governing political leadership in the Congress and Executive should not be held accountable for economic conditions.

TRANSCENDING "SUPPLY-SIDE" PRIMITIVISM

If a group of people lived in an isolated area and were faced with decisions on production and consumption, wouldn't it be likely that they would try to identify the main needs of the group and then set up priorities on the basis of what is most needed and most urgent?

The next likely question would be: Who should do what? Surely there would be plenty for everyone to do, but a division of labor would be necessary. The one question that would be most absurd would be, "What level of unemployment should we have, and who should be unemployed?"

Yet that absurd question has been asked and answered for many years by the executive branch of our federal government. The *need* to have *unemployment* has been accepted, for the presumption was that if you had too much employment you would have too much inflation (The Phillip's Curve) and so the question has always been, should there be 4, 5, 6, 7, 8, 9, or 10 percent unemployment? Reagan was willing to let unemployment go to virtually any level because he focused primarily on reducing inflation, and was willing to pay the price of unemployment, which rose as high as 50 percent of the workforce in some small towns and among particular groups such as black youth.

Many people are shocked to find out what is common knowledge among students of government, namely, that *unemployment in the United States is planned*. This country can do what was illustrated above in the plans of the "isolated" group. It can have *any* level of employment from zero to 100 percent. Jobs are human inventions. A billion Chinese could create a billion jobs and 230 million Americans can create whatever number of jobs are desired, if that is the plan. Or, there can be 10 percent unemployment, millions in compulsory exclusion from making a living—if *that* is the plan.

Why should a government create compulsory unemployment? First it is because employment is not considered as important as other goals; secondly, it is presumed that you cannot have full employment without also having inflation. The Reagan administration was willing to risk a depression to reduce inflation, even though a depression involves high unemployment. Many questioned whether the cure was worse than the illness, for one would hardly advocate that a cure for cancer would be to give strychnine to the patient.

What is not revealed to the public is that the win/lose choice of inflation or jobs results from a willful decision not to manage the economy. Therefore, to protect unregulated corporate enterprise, we create a dilemma that pits one group against another—those who profit from inflation versus those who derive income from secure employment.

After World War II and the mid-70s, Congress passed employment legislation to stimulate jobs through gorvernment spending, but there has never been a right to a job in the United States in the same legal sense as there has been a right to a basic education. Corporations have been encouraged by law to hire more minorities and young people, cities have often created jobs during summer months and provided subsidy for employers hiring young people, CETA programs have helped train young people, but having steady work is not a right in the competitive market. It is, instead, a matter of sinking or swimming. During wartime and during periods when the Democratic party was in control and supporting more public programs, more people were swimming. Though the Roosevelt administration had cut drastic unemployment levels in half, it was World War II that *eliminated* the structural unemployment of the 1930s. War expenditure has since been politically acceptable by both parties as a way of creating jobs within the military, in the military-industrial complex, and through secondary multipliers, those who sell goods and services to people spending Pentagon money. But economists found out during the 1960s that modern military spending is a low Keynesian multiplier for the creation of jobs while also producing the least desirable social products, contributing to inflation and depleting resources.[2]

In an unpopular war such as the Vietnam conflict, the President and the Congress did not think the public would support a pay-as-you-go policy, and payment was made after the war, largely through inflation. When energy prices, through real and contrived shortage (OPEC and Big Oil) and housing speculation added to inflation, the number one political concern became inflation. Then unemployment rates increased, and the dominant policy under all administrations of the 1970s was that since it was a choice between inflation *or* high employment, inflation would get first attention. What happened was that the cruelest of possible worlds resulted, with *both* increased inflation and unemployment. Inflation subsided under the Reagan administration as the economy was brought into a depression, aided by a worldwide oil glut that was an unpredicted accident not connected to Reaganomics.

With mortgage loan interest rates in double digits, unemployment the highest in forty years, burgeoning bankruptcy and business failure, and minorities losing ground, neo-classical economics is now in a sorry state. Meanwhile, supply-side economists continue to claim that there is nothing wrong with their theories, they just haven't been tried long enough.

Such behavior has not been the result of lack of alternatives; there have been alternatives, but they have been carefully ignored, *because they do not conform to ideology supported by dominant economic groups. Alternative solutions threaten the privileged positions of the more powerful and wealthy members of society, and they also lie outside the economic myths that Americans have come to accept.* The economic crises that Americans face are largely of our own making, especially so under Reaganomics, for when there is a dedication to making sure that government will not work to guarantee employment or prevent depression, these results are not surprising.

The United States has one of the lowest levels of democratic control of the economic system in the industrial world. This has resulted in a low level of distribution fairness as well as a low level of productivity. The high job security of Japanese workers has increased their enthusiasm, their loyalty, and the quality of their product, in all three of these areas eclipsing the American worker. In West Germany, democratic participation of unions on corporate boards has helped produce high levels of cooperation between labor and management, has lowered the incidence of strikes, and has raised production and product quality.

The United States has no explicit industrial policy, no distribution policy, no employment policy; the usual political behavior is *ad hoc* re- action to crises. Yet for many, freedom *from* public planning is still view- ed as a supreme value, worth fighting and dying for. Fortunately this group is shrinking and sounding more and more detached from the age in which we live. As we see the impact of our lack of planning on peo- ple, on the environment, and on our legacy to future generations, even businesses are increasingly asking for more stability and predictablity, which cannot be achieved without economic planning in the public sector.

To get the United States out of the depression, the government is currently relying on mystical forces of progress. But there is no reason why the national and world depression cannot continue if no political initiatives are taken. There is no divine intervention to save people from obsolete economic rules.

The kind of economic fundamentalism we see in much American economic ideology, especially in conservatism, is like religious fun- damentalism, based on a presumption of noncontextual absolute truth which cannot be tested. In the name of "realism" it turns the practical traditions of American "know how" upside down, and substitutes faith for problem solving.

Moving to a responsible and effective form of economics requires "demythologizing" the economic beliefs we now operate upon and ex- amining the kinds of economic rules which will provide a sustainable maximum common quality of life.

FACT AND FICTION: THE UNITED STATES ECONOMY

Myth:	*Fact:*
1. Unemployment is accidental.	Unemployment is intentional.
2. Prices are determined by the market.	Some prices are market deter- mined—many are administered by large oligopolistic corpora- tions.
3. The government breaks up monopoly.	Since the Sherman Anti-Trust Act, economic power has continued to be more concentrated in fewer corporations.

Myth:	*Fact:*
4. Large industries are the best hope for future jobs.	Large industries use increasingly fewer people; small businesses are the growing areas of employment, but often with low pay and low security.
5. Wages are based on marginal contributions—people get what they contribute.	Wages are often a function of power of the corporation to pass on wage increases to consumers through higher prices.
6. Managerial salaries are determined by personal contributions and competition.	Managerial salaries are often self-established by in-group power, much as congressional salaries are established by congressmen.
7. Professionals such as lawyers and doctors compute their fees according to the cost of their education and the importance of their social contribution.	Lawyers and doctors have used power to form unions called professions, which engage in the elimination of competition through monopoly and price control to maximize fees.
8. The control of inflation requires a monetary policy which necessarily brings an economy to the brink of depression.	Microcontrols that focus on specific wage, price, and resource areas can achieve real growth and full employment without destructive inflation, if there is strong public support.
9. Prices are based on costs of production plus a fair profit mark-up.	Prices have no necessary connection to costs. They are based on "all the market will bear." (See #5, 6, 7.)
10. Most people living in poverty in the United States are unemployed.	Most people living in poverty in the United States are employed and underpaid.
11. Most of the unemployed and the poor are minorities.	Most of the unemployed and the poor are white.
12. Women receive equal pay for equal work.	Women on the average receive about 73 percent of the pay of men for equal work.
13. People are paid according to what they contribute.	People are usually paid at the lowest price producers can get workers to accept. When pay rises, it usually rises because of unionization or in-group power.

Myth:

Fact:

14. Natural resources can be obtained when shortage occurs by the use of capital to obtain more of the resources.

Geology wins out over economics—scarcity can be absolute. Obtaining more of a scarce, hard to find resource (like oil) increasingly moves to a point at which costs exceed the value of the product.

15. Economic ideology comes from the will of the people and is freely chosen.

Most economic ideology comes from a narrow range of ideas permeating mass media, advertising, schools, businesses, families, professions, and professional economists.

16. Americans can choose economic ideology while Russian people have no choice.

Russian people have explicit ideological control, and most of them know it. Americans have implicit ideological control and most of them do not know it and are unaware of alternatives.

17. American political/economic ideology is the most liberal and humanitarian in the world.

Among the industrial democracies, America has the most conservative political/economic ideology.

18. In the United States, the public interest controls economic behavior.

The United States has less public guidance of economic behavior than any of the industrial democracies.

19. Military spending stimulates the American economy and produces jobs.

Military spending depresses the American economy and produces a loss of total jobs.

20. The GNP has risen most in those countries that have large military expenditures.

The GNP has risen most in those countries with small military expenditures, such as Japan and Sweden. England and the United States have high military expenditures and low GNP increase.

21. Pollution is an "externality" unrelated to economics.

Pollution adds to profit because it is a way of getting people other than the producer to pay for the "garbage" resulting from production. Pollution is always subsidized.

22. Pollution in moderate amounts will help add to the production and prosperity of an economy.

Pollution aids individual producers and always depresses the total real economic system, for the

Myth:	Fact:

| | costs (sickness, escape from cities, reviving rivers, killing fish, etc.) are always greater to the total society than prohibitions at the source of pollution. |
| 23. Environmentalist action has a net effect of producing a decline in employment; environmentalists are, therefore, foes of working class people. | Most environmental action has *added* to employment, requiring more pollution equipment, a more labor intensive economy with appropriate technology, renewable forms of energy, and reclamation of industry. Environmental laws protect health and safety of industrial workers. |

DEFINING NEW STANDARDS AND INDICATORS

After demythologizing comes redefinition, and one of the first things we need to do is reexamine the indicators that are used to decide what is happening, whether it is good or bad, and who receives the "goods," and who the "bads."

Indicators are measurement devices, and like other instruments of measurement—IQ tests, automobile horsepower, personal wealth—they have provided a convenient and simple quantitative measurement which makes them attractive devices. But it is an old story among measurement specialists that when you let the convenience of measurement instruments become too dominant you begin to change the thing being measured in order to fit the measurement standards. Then means determine the ends.

This process, along with the old bookkeeper way of thinking about an economy, GNP, per capita income, and monetary theory, has provided us with an obsolete definition of economic values. By these conventional standards, the economy could be seen as improving when on the basis of quality of life standards, it could actually be regressing. Conversely, when indicators go down, quality of life may really be going up.

Some of the leading current indicators are consumer prices, housing starts, retail sales, industrial production, unemployment rate, stock market movement, balance of trade, GNP, and per capita income. These are all unreliable indicators when they are given only quantitative measurements. Let us examine housing, industrial production, and employment to illustrate.

Consider housing starts. Should we merely count numbers of housing units as we usually do, or should we indicate the income level of the people getting housing and whether they really need it or not? After all, the units might be second homes for the rich in resort areas. Should we identify how they are made—to self-destruct, to waste heat? Should we see if they have been located on prime topsoil where the resource depletion may offset the housing advantage? And most of all, why should we care about housing starts when many older houses can be remodeled and large houses divided into units to supply more housing? Clearly, this indicator does not address the most important question, namely, is housing being improved through responsible forms of construction and development for those who really need better housing? We could rejoice, looking at indicators, when we really need to despair.

Consider industrial production. This indicator calculates units of increase in dollar amounts. But what is being produced? Is it bombs? Nuclear missiles? Gas-guzzling cars? Carcinogenic cigarettes? Saturday night special handguns? Medical expenditure for cancer and bullet wounds? Chain saws to cut down the last of the unprotected ancient redwoods?

Clearly, what is being produced, the relationship of such production to human need, and the loss through pollution "externalities" currently not counted as costs, need to be the real considerations. Industrial production is also a deceptive indicator, for quantitative profits can be directly connected with qualitative losses.

The unemployment rate is particularly deceptive. This is the amount of unemployment reported when people contact a public agency to indicate they are unemployed and want a job and/or public assistance. Many unemployed people have given up looking for a job. They are often the people most in despair, but they are not quantified and fed back into the indicator. If enough people live with a sense of hopelessness and do not resort to public agencies, the indicator will show progress because the "unemployment rate" will be low.

When statistical quantification is made sufficiently obscure to the public and used in a Machiavellian manner by each interest group, we have obsolete indicators serving questionable purposes, and economics truly does become the "dismal science"—or worse.

A first step in the transformation of standards and indicators is to take account of a broader range of economic values. The conventional bookkeeper approach may record costs in the production of chemicals and also profits on a conventional debits and assets sheet. But pollutants sent into the air and the toxic wastes contaminating water may not appear on the ledger sheet even though health and the quality of life are affected. These are known as *external* costs. They are external to the producer but internal to the larger society. From the standpoint of the producer, profits may exceed costs. From the standpoint of the society, costs may exceed aggregate private profits. The cost effects on health from polluted air and water and the long-term loss of valuable surface and underground water sources could be very high indeed.

When we add social and ecological costs such as the effects of noise, smelly air, tension and congestion from traffic, fear of theft and mugging, threat of job loss, destruction of natural beauty, overload of perceptual stimulus in an increasingly complicated world, sickness from environmental conditions, death from environmental factors, the real costs become enormous.

When these kinds of costs are subtracted from conventional benefit indicators, the evidence for depression and regression of the economy becomes even greater. No one would ask for more of the same if the status quo was perceived to be a loser rather than a winner. But increasingly we have been engaging in this kind of self-deception.

There is nothing wrong with progress, if the general quality of life really improves. There is a great deal wrong with the way economics is played if we manipulate the standards and indicators so that the lights flash on and say we are winners, when in fact we are losers.

The human tendency to scapegoat economic problems instead of designing an improved economy is an obstacle that will not easily go away. We are ready to blame "the high cost of government," "communism," "the Russians," "the liberals," "welfare bums," "unions," "blacks," "lazy people," "capitalists," instead of planning to reshape the system.

When we prevent people from considering systematic economic alternatives, we paralyze their capacity to choose. The presumption of *economic determinism*, meaning the market guided by immutable laws of supply and demand, is the most effective way to block the creative redesign of the economic system. People then become bystanders, observing economic forces over which they have no control. As bystanders, we see the "light at the end of the tunnel," and we are sure the recession is ready to "bottom out." Business cycles are presumed to be natural ups and downs, and the clever and successful person is the one who forecasts the market correctly and buys and sells appropriately during those ups and downs.

If we decide to control economics instead of being controlled by economic myths, we must learn to design futures within the framework of what is, in fact, economically, geologically, and biologically possible. We need to come to terms with the question of values and priorities and the issue of self-interest versus the public interest. If we determine that economics is to be ethics-centered instead of self-interest centered, we have taken the first big step in economic design. This requires a publicly regulated economy with explicit ethical values.

Economic profit and economic efficiency should not be primary. What should be primary is the *common quality of life.* By "common" we mean a "fair" distribution of opportunities and values. "Quality of life" includes goods, services, social environment, and biological environment as they contribute to the well being and development of a human being. If this generation lives at the expense of the next generation, the economy is unethical and based on generational exploitation. Examples of this would be not only the destruction of nonrenewable resources such as topsoil and wilderness, but also such actions as the failure to provide maintenance of roads, water systems, and sewage systems, thereby allowing huge maintenance costs to accumulate over the heads of the young.

Economics should include the home economy. If people are able to raise food on their own property they do not need some of the income others use to travel to the store to buy food. Per capita income, therefore, is not a good indicator of quality of life. If people repair their own houses, they do not need the income needed to hire repair people, and the loss of income to the repair people can be balanced off with their doing similar things such as fixing their own cars and not being dependent on commercial maintenance. When food is prepared at home, people do not need the money that would be paid for restaurant food. All these things add to the real income of people, and are not taxed. So a penny saved is a penny-and-a-half or two pennies earned. Similarly, in the conservation of energy, oil that is saved is economically equal to oil that is produced. Neither neo-classical nor Keynesian economists factor in the home economy and the conservation economy, thus omitting crucial indicators applicable even to GNP. Twenty-first century economics, if it is based on common quality of life, needs to factor in a much wider set of considerations so that money acquired through the exchange of goods and services is only a part of the economic product.

The choice is either to let economics be defined in the conventional way and then to say that economics is to become less and less important to human life, or to broaden its definition so that economics increases in importance because it includes social and environmental costs and benefits.

In this new economics, both the processes and products become relevant. If people in a factory produce good products but do so in noisy, autocratic, alienating, monotonous conditions, this micro-unit of the economy is providing pluses in products, but minuses in effects on the people who are producing. Fortunately, we do not have to choose between good processes or good products. Sweden, Japan, and West Germany have increased both the quantity and the quality of products through employee participation in production and management policies. Cooperation between employees takes them away from the isolated conditions of old-style production lines. Feedback from consumers to producers increases the sense of responsibility for high quality.

None of this is new in theory, and Americans, in fact, created much of the theory, proposing democratic procedures for business as they did for education. But the hierarchical structure of American businesses has encouraged American managers to largely ignore these procedures. Ironically, a professor of business from the United States, Douglas McGregor, went to Japan, *after American businesses rejected him*, and became the leading theorist of change in Japanese business toward greater intrinsic satisfaction in work and greater product quality.[3]

ECONOMICS AND HUMAN DEVELOPMENT: WE BECOME WHAT WE DO

Aside from product output, the success of an economy needs to be measured by indicators that take account of the effects of economic processes on people. Has the work contributed to the human development of a person or has it degraded him? Has there been democratic, participatory experience that will help the person be a better citizen in a democratic society, or is the work structure class-stratified and autocratic? Is there honest and accurate use of information or propagandistic manipulation of people through "public relations" and "personnel management" which treats people as objects and instruments rather than as human beings? And conversely, is an employee carrying out an obligation to do good work and also contributing to good social relations with the others he works with?

The most civilized and mature level of economic planning requires not only consideration of goods and services, but consideration of the human development effects of economic activity.

Economic activity occupies much of a person's life, and our personalities are largely shaped by environments and tasks, many of which are economic. This is true for both the producer and consumer who experience the symbols, sounds, sights, beliefs, work roles, authority structures, and technology of an economic environment.

Currently we have many people creating advertising to get consumers to buy goods. Much of the advertising tries to manipulate the consumer without revealing significant information about the product. It is, therefore, propaganda. In turn, the consumer is deluged with sounds and sights along the streets and highways, on radio and TV, and in newspapers and journals. Not all advertising is exploitative; some is informative. But the experience for both the producer of exploitative forms of advertising and for the consumer is *miseducational*. If a plan were to be developed explicitly to use communication to cripple the intellectual and emotional aspects of human development, a better model would be hard to find.

The appeal to bad judgment in most advertising reveals that the producer has little to offer in the way of either a new product or one with significant advantages over others. Contemporary Americans live in the middle of this sensory and symbolic bombast, revealing itself so ubiquitously that although the isolation of hills and forests promises an attractive chance of escape, even there an aircraft sky-writer selling a soft drink might appear.

At the minimum, this innundation of silly and degrading "messages" makes sensible human development difficult. At the maximum, it cripples the minds of many people who may never be able to think clearly or sensitively while living in a social environment that makes every attempt to manipulate behavior without regard for truth. Children are sent to schools, ostensibly to learn to think clearly and to honor truth, but for many young people, the influence of advertising exceeds the influence of conventional schooling. A good school will help young people analyze the exploitative and deceptive aspects of advertising. But exposure to such analysis in today's schools is not a common educational experience.

When economics is understood to have such enormous influence over human development, we will have to treat the economic institutions themselves as educational influences in which not only advertising but the human organization of humans for economic tasks becomes educational or miseducational. In a technological society such as ours, we often treat technology and organization as value neutral, mere "technique." But organizational structure and advertising are not value neutral—constituting much of our environment and culture. They influence ideology and they shape human values. The symbols, beliefs, habits and attitudes within our minds come mainly from our experience with the particular environment that constitutes our culture; and the culture of business, unions, and commercialism is a producer of *people*, not merely of goods and services.

Commerce, as it is now organized in the United States, is a promoter of hedonism and personal greed justified under the rubric of "freedom." Such freedom applies to the advertiser who is free to bombard us with messages to serve his purposes, but it does not include our freedom to drive along the highway or through a city without having our view of the landscape obscured by advertising. It does not include the freedom to hear television programs uninfluenced by the profit seeking and the ideology of advertisers, or even to hear advertiser approved programs without continual interruption by commercials. (Even *public* television in the United States is economically supported and ideologically influenced by private sponsors.)

It is remarkable that Americans have tolerated the miseducation and ugliness of rampant commercialism for so long. The more advanced and civilized areas of the United States have taken steps to control freeway signs, and a few cities effectively control the size of city advertising signs. By contrast, Las Vegas is Exhibit A in ugliness through garish visual advertising. Regulation of advertising in the twenty-first century can go either in the direction of Las Vegas or in the direction of states that prohibit obtrusive signs. These are two different conceptions of freedom and two different ways of thinking about the impact of environmental economics on human development.

The economy takes its major toll, especially in the workplace, where working people are still often treated as commodities or parts in a production line. There has been significant progress in the last century; work weeks have been somewhat shortened, unions have helped establish grievance procedures for blue-collar workers, and even teachers and airline pilots have come to use union services. The environment of the workplace has generally improved and there is more sensitivity about human relations; but there is also a faster pace and other stresses.

Much of the improvement came from labor shortages resulting from growth economics, especially in the 1960s. The Vietnam War temporarily stimulated the economy as had World War II, thus strengthening the bargaining power of wage and salary earners. Not everything will be lost through the depression of the early 1980s, but labor progress will backslide as high unemployment produces labor surpluses and loss of worker power.

Here are examples of goals for a human development economy of the twenty-first century, taken from small-scale experiments already underway.

1. Flexible work times and work periods are needed so that people can work longer hours four days a week and have three days off; work shorter hours for six days, if they like; begin late in the day, avoiding traffic; or work half time at their own option. Some states (Hawaii, for example) have rules for teachers that permit voluntary half-time teaching, thus providing two jobs for people who prefer half-time jobs. Flexible work time has double payoff, for the employee and for the employer. Better working conditions can serve in lieu of higher pay and provide better output, as the energies and morale of employees are increased.

2. Vacations in the United States have been among the shortest of industrial countries. Workers in France have six weeks vacation per year; even Germany under Hitler provided most people with four weeks vacation a year, more time that most workers now have in the United States, forty-five years later. Sabbaticals and exchanges, already a tradition among university professors and teachers, need to be spread to all fields of work, so that every six or seven years workers can take an extended leave of a few months, providing it is directed toward experiences that are likely to contribute to their growth and development. Various kinds of travel, education, and creative projects could qualify. Sabbaticals plus expanded vacation times with more planning options by the employee would make one's workplace a less dominating and oppressive part of life, and people would work with associates who would be involved in a greater variety of experiences in addition to their work. Instead of being anxious to retire as soon as one can afford to, such employees could mix leisure, education, and activities with work and make their employed years more attractive.

3. Within the workplace there is clear need for greater participation in understanding and shaping the institution. Chinese and Japanese workers provide examples that Americans need to consider, for they meet to discuss ways to improve work and work conditions. Alienation of workers from their economic institution insures low quality work, absenteeism, and costly labor conflict. It also deprives the economic system of the creative intelligence of

most of the workforce, when people are treated as mere mechanical producers. Autocratic arrogance of many American managers leads them to believe that only they are the producers of ideas while the work force is merely an implementer. But human intelligence at all levels should contribute to better goods, services, and a human work environment.

4. The humanization of the economic system may not always provide an economic payoff. Though product and service quality and new ideas will generally increase through greater humanization of work, it may not justify higher pay. If Americans wish to become "economic animals," as the Japanese often call themselves, they can increase their output and demand higher pay. But if demands for efficiency and productivity are too extreme, economics will control people, and other human values will be lost. Much of the high per capita income of industrial nations has been based on the "energy slaves" of fossil fuels and machines. As the oil era comes to an end, per capita production will no longer continue to increase at the same rate. There can even be decline. But if quality of life is the primary goal rather than monetary per capita income, real progress can continue as total standards of living increase through the humanization of the economic system. In such a world people may not have the money to fly to Europe for their two-week vacation, but they can instead spend a month camping, fishing, and being at home with their family. They can attend universities with pay through their sabbaticals and have time to participate in politics and in the life of their community. They then become egalitarian aristocrats making valuable use of leisure and helping to build a better society while the simple-minded monotony of repetitious work is increasingly turned over to machines and electronic devices.

All this has already started, but it is in danger of backsliding under administrations such as the Reagan administration which give priority to the "market" instead of to human development. Real progress will require stronger political assistance to manage an economy that serves people instead of merely using them. Job insecurity under high unemployment is the main threat, for producers increase their power over people when there is a labor surplus. Economic humanization requires either a labor shortage or democratic control of the economy.

Many people feel today that their labor is producing largely trivial or useless products, often poorly made; and many people know that through production of war products they are contributing to death and destruction. The only satisfaction for such people is the extrinsic reward—the money earned.

But the person who provides useful goods and services at fair prices has a basis for intrinsic satisfaction as well as a double payoff, a sense of the importance of the work being done *and* the money earned. In addition, if the work is interesting, involving new learning and creative challenge, there is a triple payoff.

When distribution fairness is considered, we must take into account all three of the above work values: money, social value, intrinsic interest. The maldistribution is now extreme—the highest paid people have the most interesting jobs, the lowest paid usually the least interesting. Many of the highest paid, however, are involved in producing wasteful, shoddy, trivial products. High-income professionals and executives are often designing and producing war products, the technology of death.

People working toward contributions that serve human need, contribute to a peaceful world, and respect nature would have a form of "payment" that the work of the twenty-first century should include. When we understand that the environment of work and the purposes it serves affect our mind, our senses, and our moral and ethical development, we must treat the economic system as a socializing system, shaping human personality. Evaluation of an economy on the basis of dollar output and GNP, excluding human development economics, is both outmoded and barbaric.

The Right to Work

Unionization responded to the job insecurity of the 1930s by producing contracts with higher levels of job security and legal procedures for grievances. Yet the high unemployment of the 1980s reveals that we still need to have a higher level of job security and a broader choice of jobs available. One of the remaining barbarisms of current economics, a residue of nineteenth century capitalism, involves the "right" of economic managers to unemploy people but does not include the "right" to be employed.

Employment has profound meaning to a member of a society. It is economic *and* psychological. It means the person is a contributing member, deserving respect from others and entitled to self-respect. But the right to particular employment must be based on the capacity to do the work either initially or through training.

Our economy today is a minefield of discriminatory obstacles. Groups such as unions engage in self-protection; professionals use their collective power to enhance their status and their pocketbooks. The demands of women to equal treatment have revealed how men have falsified many qualification requirements, even physical requirements. Some jobs do require considerable strength which may exceed the capacity of half of the men and three-fourths of the women, but a strong woman should not be excluded by categorical qualifications used for exclusionary discrimination.

Nor should the *route* to qualifications such as credentialing be unfairly exclusionary. Professions usually require university degrees that protect the turf claimed by the professionals. Nurses should be aided in having the opportunity to become doctors, teacher aids to become teachers, and legal clerks to become attorneys. Job qualifications should really be justified by the requirements of the job. Though the United States has a comparatively good record in providing college education for low-income citizens, the costs of education still exclude millions of people who would benefit both themselves and society if higher education and training were economically possible for them. Recent reductions in federal aid to higher education and student loans exacerbate this condition. The GI Bill, following World War II, was a significant developer of people's abilities through education, and many who are now talented and contributing members of the economy were aided by that opportunity.

The autonomy of professional groups has been granted by law and custom, providing the group establishes standards that protect the public. However, because of lack of public scrutiny and power over the profession, the rules are often rigged to provide special status and income for professionals. Professors in professional schools serve as gatekeepers and controllers of standards, yet once they have authorized someone to enter a profession, there is no longer serious evaluation of the utility of the university requirements, and so the gatekeepers disconnect their requirements from public accountability.

Law is a case in point. The law is actually "owned" by the public; it is public policy created by representatives paid by the public, yet lawyers have incrementally increased their power to interpose themselves between the citizen and the law, greatly to their economic advantage. By engaging in fee monopoly (recently declared illegal), by having tight exclusion of people practicing law, by maximizing obfuscation, by restricting access to courts and allowing judges who are themselves attorneys to establish attorney court fees, they have transformed law practice into a service for the rich, even though a vastly larger public needs legal assistance.

We are being told that there will soon be too many lawyers. Perhaps so, but at current fee levels, most of the public will continue to be unable to obtain legal services. Para-legal services have begun which employ many people without as yet threatening the legal profession, but employment frontiers have been barely explored. We need to demystify the field of law, put it into the service of the public, and allow it to generate many needed jobs.

Community mediation services, now being developed, can use educated lay people to solve many disputes at a pre-judicial level, helping to unclog courts and reduce legal costs. Public funds for legal aid have helped the poor obtain legal assistance they would otherwise not have had, and many class action cases have been won on behalf of the poor in the fields of housing and jobs.

The current medical profession is equally culpable. An organized union has established political control of medical licensing and fees so that American medicine is the most costly in the world, American doctors the highest paid, and access to American medical schools based heavily on one's economic capacity, usually through family, to finance a long period of formal education.

The exponentially increasing costs of medical care along with exponentially increasing costs in military spending are becoming economically untenable. In the medical area the time is ripe for integrated planning. We might begin by avoiding calling medical care "health care." Health care, using the growing evidence about the relationship between health and environment (food, smoking, workplace, air, water) can significantly reduce the need for medical care. If health were the central planning goal, most medical care could be eliminated, for heart disease, diabetes, and cancer can be reduced enormously by environment changes. An economy aimed at health would be able to open up a great variety of jobs in preventive medicine, diet, and recreation. Health education, environmental control of public and workplace standards, and agriculture that produces high nutrition, low-fat, chemically uncontaminated foods, could provide a drastic reduction in illness and result in economic savings that would underwrite many jobs connected with social needs.

Ironically, under today's deceptive economic indicators, the increase in medical costs contributes to a high GNP and provides a signal indicating "progress." Under quality of life indicators, it would signal *regression.*

Job creation and economic reform should be tied to economic goals that focus on a high common quality of life with designated priorities. When basic human needs, which constitute human rights, are made clear, they should be put into basic law, preferably constitutional law.

Then an orderly and rational way of planning employment can be developed. After human and material resources are allocated to basic human needs, the growing threat of polluted drinking water, the depletion of topsoil threatening future food production, the lack of adequate housing and transportation, the lack of health services and equal educational opportunity can all be targeted for job creation. Microplanning by government, using tax encouragements and attractive loans, can be used to aid the private sector. But when jobs are not available through the private sector, government must be ready to provide them through tax monies, if there is to be an effective right to employment.

Converting from a war economy to a peace economy and from a petroleum economy to a sustainable solar-based economy can create an enormous number of jobs. Even from an economic standpoint, ignoring the humanitarian factor, it is much too costly for a nation to have large numbers of people unemployed and not making an economic contribution. The economic cost to a nation is always a function of its tax base and a Reagan depression which weakens the tax base and leaves many people unemployed increasingly hinders our capacity for providing employment opportunities and basic needs for everyone. With full employment opportunities, flexible work weeks, and opportunity to obtain retraining for better jobs, the tax costs for maintaining full employment can be borne by a nation because so many people will be contributing to the economy. The successful industrial nations have known this for years, and have used taxes and regulation to their advantage, but the message has been slow to get across the ocean. Lester Thurow points out that: "Government absorbs slightly over 30 percent of the GNP in the United States, but over 50 percent of the GNP in West Germany. Fifteen other countries collect a larger fraction of their GNP in taxes. . . . Ours is not the economy with the most rules and regulations; on the contrary, it is one with the fewest rules and regulations. . . . It simply isn't possible to fire workers abroad as it is here. It is a dubious achievement, but nowhere in the world is it easier to lay off workers."[4]

The Cost of a War Economy

For the last three decades the military has been the largest single source of economic demand in the United States. An estimated 28,000 jobs are created for each billion dollars of military spending, but funds spent for the military are withdrawn from other sectors. Approximately fifty-seven thousand jobs are created when a billion dollars is used for personal consumption. And 70,000 jobs would be created if the money were spent on education.[5]

This means about 42,000 more jobs per billion of dollars of expenditure would be created if the funds were spent on education rather than the military. Therefore, a military budget of $100 billion would produce a reduction of 42,000 times 100 or 4.2 million jobs lost by directing the spending for the military instead of for education. Since current military spending is well over $200 billion, we can see that it is possible to account for nearly all of the current unemployment through the depressing economic effects of military expenditure over other uses.

The graphs on the following pages illustrate the economic price the United States has paid for being the highest military spender of the Western nations. Figures are listed in GDP, Gross Domestic Product, which excludes international trade. Notice the record of countries that have been low in military spending.[6]

The costs of the military are actually much larger than indicated in official budgets, which omit many costs connected with a military establishment. These include: veteran's benefits, debt interest, foreign military aid, nuclear weapons costs, the military portion of NASA, the costs of education for children living with armed forces personnel, the military related aspects of the Coast Guard and the Maritime Administration. This total military cost came to 48.6 percent of the federal budget in 1981, and current official plans for expanding the military would cost 59.2 percent of the federal budget in 1986.[7]

The military funds are taken from domestic social needs, especially the politically weak—minorities, the young, the old, and the poor. Payment for such a huge military system either comes from inflationary expansion of the money supply or from Treasury notes that compete for capital investment funds in the market. Interest rates are forced up while capital is directed away from the private sector.

Though military expenditures are largely an economic liability, those who think they are essential for national security would say that the cost is justified. However, since national security cannot be secured by military violence in the nuclear age, the result is a double loss in both national security and economic strength. The real security of a nation is both internal and external. The road the United States has been taking threatens internal security by undermining the economy, leading us toward nuclear war internationally.

America's future depends on transition from a war economy to a peace economy. Political movements to substantially reduce armaments

FIGURE 4.1 Military Spending as a Share of GDP, Selected Nations, 1960–80

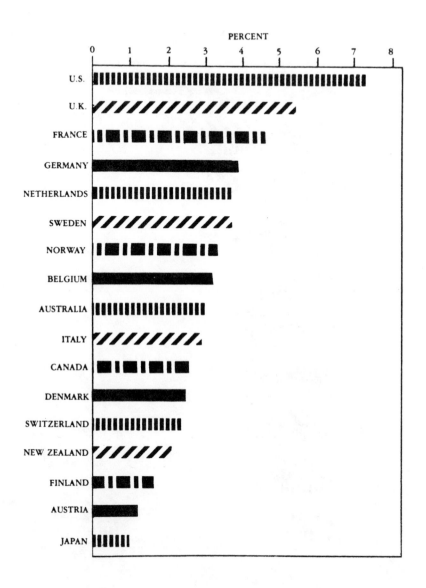

Note: The United States and Britain have been the highest military spenders. Figures 4.1 - 4.4 reproduced from *Military Expansion, Economic Decline* by Robert W. De Grasse, Jr., 1983, pp. 77, 81–83, by permission from the Council on Economic Priorities.

FIGURE 4.2 Manufacturing Capital Growth, Selected Nations, 1960–73, 1960–78, 1973–78

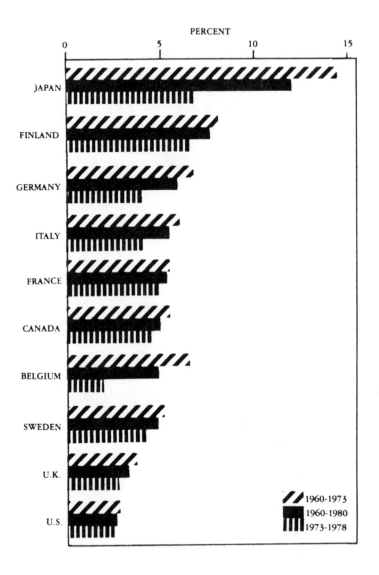

Note: The United States and Britain have had the lowest capital growth.

FIGURE 4.3 Productivity Growth in Manufacturing Industries, Selected Nations, 1960–73, 1960–81, 1973–81

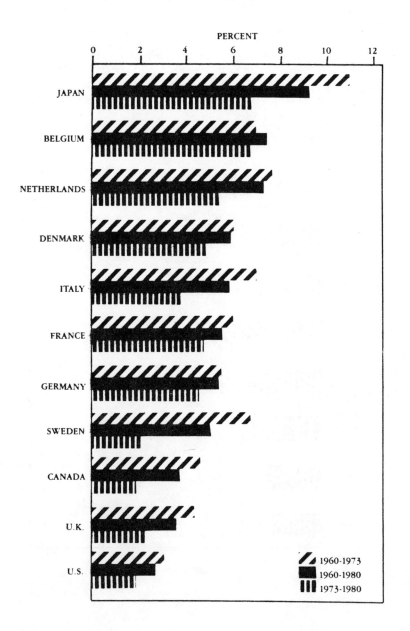

Note: The United States and Britain have had the lowest industrial productivity growth.

FIGURE 4.4 Unemployment Rate, Selected Nations, 1973–81.

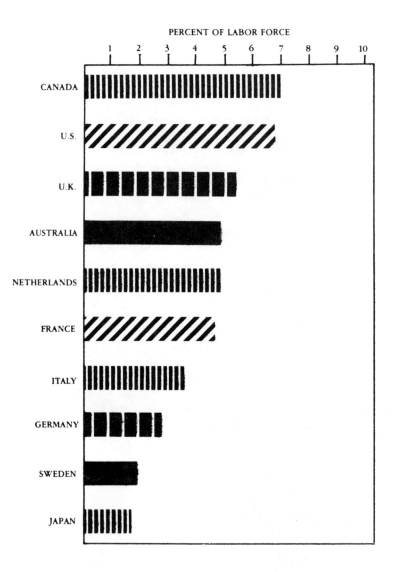

Note: The United States, Canada, and Britain have had the highest unemployment.

will not succeed until conversion of the international war system and conversion of the domestic economy are undertaken simultaneously, for they are two sides of the same coin. In the early 1970s, the State of Hawaii sponsored preliminary economic planning for conversion to a peace economy. States should take such initiatives, but federal conversion planning is the most necessary. With study and discussion of ways to move from an economy heavily involved in war production to an economy based on peaceful uses of goods and services, we would engage in the public process of designing the ways to extricate ourselves from the enormous hazards of our interdependent war-system war-economy. If people can see that new forms of planning and public policy can provide a safer more prosperous future without threatening them with employment loss, extrication from our current economy will be possible.

Ecological Economics

Ecological economics is not a matter of choice. Limited resources, a finite planet, and effects of pollution set limits that cannot be avoided if economics is to sustain human life. If these limits are violated too severely, human life cannot survive. If violation is less severe, the quality of life suffers. A high quality of life is the result of a careful blend of economic planning with environmental planning so that employment, production, and the protection of the earth are not in conflict.

Currently both capitalist and communist countries practice economics still highly exploitative of life-sustaining resources. A twenty-first century economics which worked *within* the carrying capacity of the earth would need to be much less of a goods producing economics and more of a service economics, with more of its energy supplied by renewable solar-based power. Nonrenewable resources would be used and recycled but not consumed and destroyed.

In the twenty-first century the life support system would not be up for "grabs" to serve personal desires. Society and the environment would be understood to be inseparable, and destructive attacks on the environment would require the same criminal sanctions as destructive attacks on people.

Our *quantitative* growth economics has used taxes, loans, and advertising to keep the foot on the GNP accelerator. *Qualitative* growth economics that sustained the life-support system would use taxes, loans, education, and law to direct the economy at fulfilling human needs within carrying capacity. Ecology and human rights become the first considerations;

frivolous consumption would have secondary priority and would be acceptable only to the extent that it did not violate human rights and the life-support system.

Per capita income is now heavily based on capital intensive, energy intensive production motivated by economic profit. The economist Robert Heilbroner calls this the "business civilization" and though most people have accepted such an economy as normal and permanent, Heilbroner points out that it is built on principles that assure its own demise, not for ideological reasons but for practical reasons.

Two premises of business civilization make long-term survival impossible. One is the commitment to exponential growth of production and consumption. The other is the commitment to money rather than to natural resources as the primary capital. Like the economist Schumacher, Heilbroner sees that if the supply of natural resources relies on the market principles of a business civilization, then economic growth can continue only until the resources diminish. For Schumacher this violates the very principle sacred to business, that capital should generate profits and should not be liquidated. Even for individuals, living off the interest generated by capital instead of using up capital itself can ensure long prosperity. If our planetary life-support capital consists of nonrenewable resources, minerals, a balanced atmosphere and ozone layer, and the life-support ecosystems on which all animal life depends, then these things constitute our real capital and we should be living off its interest rather than using it up.

A sustainable economic system, therefore, uses *incoming* solar-based energy and recycles nonrenewable resources in perpetuity. It adds to ecosystems only those pollutants which are consumable food to the bacteria, insects, fish, birds, and animals that can use waste from human society to sustain their ecosystems. Waste that threatens human life rather than sustains it is part of the pre-ecological economics of a growth-based business civilization. Poison pollutants of air, water, and land are by-products of such an era.

If we focus on agriculture, we see that we have a pre-ecological form of economics which requires transition to an ecological system. This means moving from an agriculture based on chemistry to one based on ecological biology, and from a heavy petroleum dependency in fuel, fertilizer, and pesticide to the use of organic fertilizer, lighter farm machinery, and biological control of pests with mixed crops and crop rotation.

Agriculture as we now practice it is rapidly depleting topsoil, killing nitrogen-fixing bacteria, and creating super-bugs through pesticide overkill. Even more, there is no direct planning of food production for human nutrition, so the land is often used to produce foods with low nutritional values or fed to animals that convert it to high-cholesterol food that undermines our health. Moreover, many farmers run down their topsoil in anticipation of selling the land for urban subdivision.

Low cost, publicly subsidized water is allocated, especially in California, to serve large farms and to make small ones economically noncompetitive, resulting in a twentieth-century exodous of small farmers into overcrowded cities. Reversals of these trends would include greater advantages in taxes and water costs to small farmers, loans for conversion to sustainable agriculture using bio-gas and organic fertilizers to produce foods high in nutrition. And if prime topsoil is zoned to agricultural use in perpetuity, there is no economic incentive to price farmland for urban use and drive out farmers, especially the more labor intensive, land-efficient small ones.

Forestry has copied farming and made similar mistakes, focusing on tree-growing profits instead of watershed management and sustainable topsoil. Erosion and overcutting have removed topsoil, simultaneously destroying many spawning grounds for fish and reducing the growth and regeneration of new trees. Generally, private corporations have a worse record, based on "cut and run," than state and federal forest services, but most public management is heavily influenced by private exploiters and is based on a narrow conception of forestry tied to conventional economics, using pressures from one administration to another to serve short-term political goals.

Ecological forestry would sustain and build topsoil, plant trees with natural species diversity, preserve watersheds for fisheries, and therefore enhance flood control, water table penetration, CO_2 absorption and oxygen release, and weather stabilization. Recreation and selective cutting could add to the employment resulting from a more labor intensive management, and provide years of employment in reforestation of abused areas.

But our methods in agriculture and forestry are not nearly as barbaric as the rules of the game for mining. These laws came from an era when the objective was to exploit the wealth of the earth as rapidly as possible. From this heritage we continue to allow mining rights to be bought and sold so that the farmer or rancher who thinks he owns the land discovers that in fact *he owns only the surface*; unless he has separate title to underground mineral rights, his land can be invaded and mined.

Public lands such as national forests and even wilderness areas are subject to similar "claims" based on one's willingness to show that a claim is being or will be worked. Fees for this instant ownership of public resources are only nominal. There are now some requirements for protection of the land during mining, but the archaic law that separates surface ownership from what is under the ground and puts minerals in the private domain for any discoverer is in need of revision. We must have a resources policy identifying renewable and nonrenewable resources and taking the latter out of the category of absolute ownership.

Absolute ownership of nonrenewable resources conflicts with the rights of future generations. Pre-ecological economics, based on individual self-interest within the rules of the market, has ignored this issue. Whoever got to a resource first and made money from it deserved to win; if future generations made the mistake of being born too late, that was simply too bad for them. Virtue lay in seeing one's opportunity, acting on it, beating out one's competitor, and winning.

A twenty-first century economy that uses nonrenewable resources without consuming them will need to apply very limited ownership claims to nonrenewable resources or else put them directly under public control and/or ownership. Irreplaceable gene pools from plants and animals, irreplaceable ecosystems such as old growth redwoods, minerals in short supply including petroleum, all these would require ownership restrictions allowing *use* but seldom permitting *consumption*. In the case of petroleum, the lubricating qualities of petroleum could be used repeatedly through recylcing. In the case of coal, limited burning could be acceptable during transition to a nonfossil fuel economy, because the supply of coal is larger than that of any other fossil fuel. But the central principle would be to move from consumption to use of nonrenewable resources during transition to a sustainable ecological economy, so that nature's capital remains for future generations.

A historic step was taken in 1969 when Congress developed the National Environmental Policy Act which provided that on federal land and projects environmental impact statements must be developed so that alternatives and consequences can be illuminated. However, although NEPA was a way of turning on the lights, it did not include sufficient indication of where we should be going. Later bills focusing on air and water pollution and toxic substances began moving us toward the specification of acceptable versus unacceptable outcomes.

The specification of priority values and goals is what is now most needed. Such an approach is very different from relying only on *participation* in development and land use decisions. When we rely on participation, we incorporate ad hoc, piecemeal processes and preclude integrated planning that serves a set of social values and goals. Mere participation invariably provides opportunity for decision makers to use the ambiguity and conflict that results from testimony from a variety of special interests as a way of making decisions favoring the politically powerful, who are usually the economically powerful as well. *Participation in the selection of the best integrated plan is different from participation in each ad hoc planning decision.*

Democratically prescribed economic values have the danger of being devoid of ecological and human rights considerations, reflecting instead the short-run interests of a majority. The challenge is to have a procedurally democratic economy and also to include human rights considerations. These considerations include moving beyond pre-ecological economics and beyond the war system and its military-industrial complex; moving to a new level of civilization and justice where the eighteenth-century conception of rights and liberties is revised to take account of new human rights which protect future generations; providing greater economic fairness; and assigning common quality of life goals within an ecologically sustainable environment.

Conclusion

Twenty-first century economics should be:

Compatible with nature.
Designed to produce goods and services that permit a quality life for everyone.
Accessible for employment so everyone can participate and everyone can benefit.
Reliable for delivery of basic needs—food, shelter, transportation, health, and education.

The United States is not leading a transition to a twenty-first century economy, for the American economy is heavily weighted toward control by large corporations which engage in planning to serve their own interests. Without public policy goals there is no basis for managing the economy through the needed transition. Wastemaking, unemployment, inflation, pollution, high inequality, low levels of job satisfaction, and the continuing destruction of resources are inherent in the current economy. High levels of crime, suicide, tension, frustration, and social disintegration are byproducts.

Transition requires a managed economy that has explicit ethical goals, including the four listed above. Transition steps to a high quality future require that such a future be designated, planned, and realized. Elements of the transition must include transition from the war system and from fossil fuel energy. Domestically, this requires transition to a peace economy; internationally, it requires world law and international peace keeping.

Incentives in the form of grants, tax advantages, and public recognition need to be combined with penalties and prohibitions. But the central motive for the transition should come from people who share the new goals and want to help build a better society. With the threat of unemployment reduced and job security increased, people can participate in long-range goals, no longer menaced by the short-run crises and uncertainties of *laissez-faire* economics or the cynical policies of corporate oligarchies.

In order to be moved to social cooperation, people must have a sense of control over the direction of the economy. Currently, our economy breeds pessimism, blame, and predation. People's lives are wasted. A new economics would treat human development—the energies, the imagination, and the affirmation of life—as central to economic enterprise.

Such economics requires political power, but the power is of little value unless the ideas and goals related to transition are shared by most of the society. Education, debate, analysis, and the study of long-range economic alternatives are required to give political parties and platforms their substance.

American politics is in crisis. It is largely obsolete and vacuous, and as a consequence, many people reject all government as futile. We cannot simply urge people to participate; a solution requires that politics and government have more substance and become more useful so that participation will be more meaningful and productive. Proposals for integrated planning in the last chapter of this book constitute an attempt to contribute to this objective.

NOTES

1. Alan Gartner, et al., *What Reagan is Doing to Us* (New York: Harper and Row, 1982).

2. Robert W. Degrasse Jr., *Military Expansion and Economic Decline* (New York: Council on Economic Priorities, 1983).

3. The following books offer additional information about American industries that created both more humane and more productive forms of management. (Both books ignore the social value of products.) John Naisbitt, *Megatrends* (New York: Warner Books, 1982) and Thomas J. Peters and Robert H. Waterman, Jr., *In Search of Excellence* (New York: Harper and Row, 1982).

4. Lester C. Thurow, *The Zero Sum Society* (New York: Basic Books, 1980).

5. De Grasse, Jr., *Military Expansion and Economic Decline*, p. 9.

6. Ibid., pp. 77–84.

7. Ibid., pp. 14–15.

SELECTED READINGS

Best, Michael H. and William E. Connolly. 1976. *The Politicized Economy*. Lexington, Mass.: Heath and Company.

Burhans, Daniel. "The Steady State" *Center Magazine* Jan/Feb, 1975: 19–24.

Daly, Herman. 1973. *Toward a Steady-State Economy*. (San Francisco: W. H. Freeman, 1973).

Domhoff, G. William. 1979. *The Powers That Be*. New York: Vintage Books.

Galbraith, John Kennth. 1975. *Economics and the Public Purpose*. New York: New American Library.

Galtung, Johan. 1980. *The North/South Debate: Technology, Basic Human Needs and the New International Economic Order*. New York: Institute for World Order, Working Paper No. 12.

Heilbroner, Robert L. 1976. *Business Civilization in Decline*. New York: W. W. Norton, 1978.

Henderson, Hazel. 1978. *Creating Alternative Futures: The End of Economics*. New York: Perigee Books.

Lekachman, Robert. 1982. *Greed is not Enough*. New York: Pantheon.

Melman, Seymour. 1974. *The Permanent War Economy*. New York: Simon and Schuster.

Sivard, Ruth. 1983. *World Military and Social Expenditures*. Leesburg, Virginia: World Priorities.

Schumacher, E. F. 1973. *Small is Beautiful*. New York: Harper Colophon.

Weaver, James H. and Jon D. Wisman, "Smith, Marx and Malthus—Ghosts Who Haunt our Future." *The Futurist* (April 1978): 93–104.

5

Integrated Planning
and Transition

TOWARD A NEW CONCEPTION OF PLANNING

If the world often seems chaotic and even insane, it is because it has no rationale, only a history. Political power is seldom guided by careful planning. The world has no planning structure and many countries, including the United States, are without national planning goals or processes.

Insects and animals are programmed genetically for survival within an ecological niche, but people are not in niches and must learn to protect their life-support system and the members of their own species. This requires not only individual learning but also institutional adaptation. The alternative is to be submerged by problems that are compounded, being based on short range, fragmented, ad hoc politics. Solutions require that we learn to use integrated long-range planning which permits us to design and realize our common future.

Lack of planning is as much of a threat to democratic nations as the wrong form of planning so characteristic of totalitarian nations. Lack of adequate public planning produces unpredictability and disorganization. Power shifts to powerful corporations, the Pentagon, and large organized special interest groups. Public problems multiply so fast that tax money cannot keep up with band-aid responses to crime, pollution, unemployment, traffic congestion, and medical costs; the problems cannot be understood and addressed without integrated planning.

The United States and the Soviet Union represent not only antagonistic superpowers that dominate much of the world, but they also represent poor examples of public planning. The United States has too little planning; the Soviet Union has the wrong kind.

There are many kinds of planning, and I would like to clarify the kind of planning that now seems to be needed. I will label it "integrated planning."

What is Integrated Planning?

The principle that "you cannot do merely one thing" applies not only to ecological problems but also to social problems. Social problems are usually so interconnected that Harrison Brown has pointed out that it is often "easier to solve ten interlocking problems simultaneously than to solve one by itself."[1]

When causes of a set of social problems are closely connected, the apparent problem may be only a symptom of common causes. Under such conditions, if we treat a symptom as an independent problem, we may only produce additional problems. Here are three examples.

1. Building massive freeways into cities as a technology to accomodate uncontrolled urban growth produces suburban sprawl, an automobile dependent transportation system, high energy consumption, smog, high costs and high accident levels, and a city soon unable to accommodate automobiles.
2. Plans to cut back on the output of a military-industrial complex without economic transition planning produces political reaction on the part of threatened labor and industry relying on military spending.
3. Successful family planning aimed at population stability usually requires economic security that is not based on the labor of one's children. Large families in developing countries are often the basis for the economic security of a family that has no assurance of other forms of security.

These are only a few examples of problems involving multiple causes and therefore solutions requiring integrated planning. However, we should not assume that everything is connected to everything and that social problems are so complex that they are unsolvable. Some problems have simple, singular causes; some can be treated symptomatically. Others, even though they are complex, can be improved by making only a few changes. If everyone in the United States had employment opportunities, the impact on crime, family disintegration, taxes, and poverty would probably be considerable.

Why Use It?

The modern world is no longer a world of small separate tribes or villages that can live independently. Economic decisions or the lack of them can have considerable effect on people. The economic policies of powerful countries and large corporations can affect people throughout the world.

Impacts on environment can be large scale, even global. Pollution of air and water can travel around the world. The entire planet can be (and is being) heated from pollutants released in a few parts of the world.

Even more, the power of new technologies—nuclear and chemical—can affect the health and survival of everyone on this planet.

Though new social, political, environmental, and technological impacts are rapidly affecting the human future, our public policies and political structures have moved much more slowly. The lag in public knowledge and institutional reform has produced a world in which most trends provide a basis for pessimism. Yet planning in which people design their common future provides a basis for optimism. We are used to designing houses and our own futures—the design of public futures only extends what we already know.

Who Should be Involved?

We need two kinds of people. Some need to be highly specialized to know what kinds of futures are actually possible. But the public, through democratic choice, should select the best of the feasible alternatives. The public needs help through upgraded education; schools, universities, newspapers, electronic media, churches, unions, businesses, clubs—all can contribute to understanding the kind of planning politics now needed. Many people need not only an understanding of planning solutions but also understanding of ways to effectively and responsibly use their political power. Citizenship education in schools needs to be substantially changed to prepare young people to become politically effective and responsible.

Part of the new education should be to understand the various myths that become major obstacles to necessary change.

Myths Contributing to Paralysis

1. *That we need only to be changing "the minds and hearts" of people to prevent war.* Major problems such as war are institutional and not simply inside people's heads.

2. *That less government and more local community will solve our problems.* What we need is analysis of particular problems to see if they actually are local,

national, or global. We often become nostalgic about a simpler period in history when we are frustrated by modern complex problems.

3. *That when official America is anticommunistic it is necessarily pro-democratic.* Ideological naivete is often used by the United States government to encourage support of fascist governments because they are anticommunist. When politics is used to support national or corporate power, there is little opportunity to consider human rights and cooperative planning. Domination and rivalry turn the world into a struggle for superiority.

4. *That democracy is the same as capitalism.* The United States has been a capitalistic democracy, while most other Western nations have combined political democracy with more economic socialism. Foreign policy tyranny results from requiring other nations to be capitalistic. Americans have yet to decide which set of values should predominate—democratic participation at both the political and economic level, or political democracy separated from the private economic power that is called capitalism.

Integrated Planning: Questions and Responses

Give an example of a change that does not require integrated planning.

Response: An ordinance passed in San Francisco and a bill passed in Oregon in 1983 required restaurants (and in San Francisco, businesses as well) to provide separate sections for smokers or else to designate the entire area as nonsmoking.

This policy did not require simultaneous planning of other objectives. It did not, for example, affect food prices, or immediately threaten jobs, although it did establish some human rights precedents that could eventually threaten the tobacco industry.

Give an example that requires integrated planning.

Response: Arms reduction connected with disarmament proposals would be resisted by workers and entrepreneurs in the military-industrial complex. To achieve significant disarmament, we will have to plan for increased nonmilitary employment and ways of shifting arms-producing factories to other products in a peace economy.

What distinctions between short- and long-run planning should be made?

Response: A short-run antipollution goal could require rapid changes in the disposal of toxic wastes. A long-run goal could change major sectors of the economy. In farming, for example, control of insects would be through biological control and genetic resistance, requiring little or no chemical pesticides, production of which produces toxic wastes. Short-run goals should stop health hazards. Long-run goals would achieve a sustainable economy working within the carrying capacity and the life support system of nature.

What distinctions should be made between minimal and maximal goals?

Response: Minimal goals would provide food and water to those who are starving. Maximal goals would aim at a worldwide high quality of life. Minimal goals would require elimination of the war system. Maximal goals would aim at high levels of world cooperation.

Why not let the market be the "planner"?

Response: The market moves goods and services to those who can pay for them. It ignores human needs. It does not distinguish between renewable and nonrenewable resources. It has no concern for future generations. It sells the technology of violence to the highest bidder. The market insures that open competition will be diminished by those with the most economic power, as a way of increasing profits. It moves inherently toward economic injustice rather than toward economic justice.

Will integrated planning result in centralized and oppressive government and loss of human freedom?

Response: Currently the freedom to survive, to have a liveable environment, and to have economic justice is already jeopardized. Planning that is unnecessarily centralized and that prevents participation could add to the current oppression. Very little that is done in the Soviet Union, for example, is an appropriate model for democratic nations. Democratic, integrated planning could increase both freedom and security by including human rights and effective means for participation.

How can it be determined whether planning should be centralized or decentralized?

Response: Planning should never be more centralized than is necessary to manage a particular problem. If the problem is national unemployment, it is tied to the national and possibly the international economy. Action by states and counties could produce only minor improvement.

Human rights are global and cannot be limited to local planning. Scarce nonrenewable resources involve common human heritage claims. But the particular esthetic character of a town or the style of life of individuals or groups, if it does not injure others, should be a matter of local choice.

Can goals be centralized and implementation decentralized?

Response: Oregon's land use plan (explained later) uses state goals and county implementation. Local situations may permit a variety of approaches to achieve goals. Transition to human rights begins at different levels of achievement throughout the world and requires local variations in rates of change.

But local authority can be used to subvert national goals, as in the case of desegregated schools. Or, on the other hand, feedback from local areas could correct requirements that are too narrow, such as the use of busing to achieve integrated schools rather than the use of greater economic equality for minorities.

Can participation be compatible with integrated planning?

Response: Yes, if there are two stages of planning. The first, development of alternative integrated plans, requires that professional and lay planners develop feasible plans. These should be subject to public criticism. But the choice of the best of these plans requires democratic participation and public acceptance.

Can participation be used to prevent integrated planning?

Response: Yes, if each issue is treated separately. Fragmentation of public issues typically sets in motion a variety of uncoordinated policies which usually emphasize short-range goals and often create as many problems as they solve. For instance, if transportation ignores land use, housing, and energy, a system of roads may result which destroys much farmland, creates urban sprawl, uses petroleum at a maximum rate, pollutes the air, and requires very high taxes. This has been the American model for the last 30 years.

Wouldn't "muddling through" be better than an overly planned society?

Response: Neither extreme is necessary. Muddling through is short range, reactive, piecemeal; overly planned societies restrict novelty and variety. But there is no reason why novelty, variety, and personal innovation cannot be planned objectives in balance with other social goals.

EXAMPLES TO BUILD ON

Kenneth Boulding has pointed out that: "Anything that is, is possible." When the question of feasibility of goals arises, one of the best ways to decide the question is to see if something similar has already been done. When a plan proposes something without precedent, we can only judge its possibilities through what we know about the natural world and human potentiality. But most integrated planning can make use of previous related achievements to stimulate imagination and suggest what is possible. Here is a set of such examples.

Early Federal Initiatives

The Congress of the United States passed the Morrill Act in 1862, providing land and funds for public higher education, especially in the area of agriculture and mechanics. Many of the state colleges and universities which have since provided liberal arts and professional education were created by this federal initiative. This was a form of early planning which had public goals and then made use of the economic means to achieve them. The entire system of public education fits into the same effort on the part of government to improve the quality of life for Americans. It should be remembered that the structure of most public education was established before the twentieth century.

The Tennessee Valley Authority was a pioneer effort by the federal government in the 1930s to develop the economy of the southern states through a network of dams, irrigation systems, and power plants. Finally, two more examples of federal initiative can be seen in the public postal system and rural electrification programs, part of the history of planning through government which added to national cohesion, rural quality of life, and economic development.

Land Use

Hawaii in 1961 established the first statewide land use policy in the United States aimed particularly at preserving prime farmland and watershed. A state board had authority to override county planning, but because the state board was appointed by the governor, political pressures soon resulted in turning over considerable farmland to development. Nevertheless, watersheds were successfully preserved because they were the sources of water vital to households and agriculture. But when uncontrolled development threatened the quality of life a new movement for planning resulted, and in 1978 Hawaii adopted a long-range state growth plan, giving more attention to carrying capacity.

A better model for land use, now the most exemplary in the United States, was created in Oregon in 1973. The Oregon plan set forth the objectives of land use planning but left the particular ways those objectives were to be achieved to the local counties. Preservation of farmland has been a major objective, but water pollution, air pollution, and even the encouragement of carefully controlled economic growth has been included. The Oregon plan, supported by the governor, the legislature, and most of the residents, has provided integrated state land use planning that has been generally effective in curtailing the urbanization of farmland while adapting state goals to all local values that were consistent with those goals.

The participation process and the implementation details were worked out until the plan was largely implemented by the end of the 1970s. Among needed priorities was farmland preservation, but procedures for adjudicating conflicts also needed to be developed. These helped bypass long, costly, and indefinite periods of appeals through the courts.

The plan progressed because it had major support of the citizenry, yet there were many people who were discontented. Some thought the plan was un-American, unconstitutional, and a destroyer of individual freedom. Three statewide referendums were held to repeal the plan and all failed. Some developers and some farmers who wanted to convert their land to development were strongly opposed to it, but they have remained a minority.

The contention that the plan had kept industry out of Oregon was investigated by the Governor's commission in 1982 and no industry was identified that had stayed away from Oregon because of the state plan. On the contrary, some companies indicated that Oregon was an attractive place for industry because the land rules were clear and well-defined and the environment was appealing as a living area for their employees.[2]

Shoreline Protection

California took the first initiative in 1972 (through Proposition 20) to control development on its coastline, much of which is one of exceptional beauty but was becoming overdeveloped. Regional land use boards planned their objectives in coordination with a state board and placed stricter control over shoreline land use. Development on shoreline land has thus been substantially controlled; however, strong reaction from developers has weakened many of the early objectives.

Hawaii copied California's shoreline protection and better control over scenic and pristine shorelines has resulted.

Within the last few years many states have created stronger control over shoreline development, though much of it arrived too late to protect natural beauty and to avoid destruction of homes built on fragile coastlines inappropriate for such development. Southern California is the most well-known example of an area with deteriorating shoreline and ecologically inappropriate development.

New Forms of Law

Hawaii's constitution provides for a state constitutional convention every ten years, if it is authorized by the public. Two new constitutions have been created since Hawaii's statehood in 1959, and the last revision produced the most progressive changes in constitutional law within the United States.

Beyond the usual emphasis limited to procedures, contractual law, and protections from government power, the Hawaii Constitution now includes considerations of environmental rights, rights of future generations, and equity rights for Hawaiians.

One provision establishes the right to a "clean and healthful environment." Constitutional rights have previously been based on protections; whereas, questions of pollution have often been decided in the political arena, weighing the power of the polluter against the power of those affected by and protesting the pollution. Such contests have been resolved through media pressure, interest groups, and political pressures which usually favor corporate power. But any constitutional right, like the First Amendment right, does not depend on the numbers of people who have such rights violated. A constitutional provision provides *prior* rights, meta-law which has more power than either a legislative bill or an administrative decision. Therefore, it indicates how a hierarchy of values can be developed which can provide ethical priorities and can control economic behavior.

The new Hawaii Constitution stipulates the following planning goals: conservation of agricultural land; encouragement of both diversified agricultural and self-sufficiency agriculture; holding in trust of public natural resources for present and future generations; provision of state power to plan and manage population growth and to protect and regulate water resources for public benefit. The constitution also includes the requirement of approval by two-thirds of both the state house and senate before nuclear power plants can be licensed.

Each county (island) as well as the state has a general plan, providing even more specificity within the framework of the new constitution to control development, population, and land use under emerging standards of carrying capacity. Honolulu in particular has been overdeveloped and its water supply and farmland threatened, and the state as a whole is highly vulnerable to international changes that could cut off food and petroleum.

These are aggressive attempts to produce integrated planning, even though emerging political pressures can still override the general plans. Yet this way of using government to plan at local and state levels is fundamentally different from the *lassez-faire* nonplanning of only 25 years ago. Unfortunately, for most mainland states such nonplanning is still the rule and they are thereby compounding their problems.

International Law

For the last 20 years one of the most encouraging proposals has been to have ocean resources dedicated to the "common heritage" and controlled by an international ocean regime under new international law. As this idea took form through a long series of meetings by nations of the world, the newly developing poor nations tried to direct this law of the oceans so that it would particularly serve poor nations by distributing the wealth of the ocean resources (mainly oil and minerals) toward nations most in need.

The United States supported this development until the time of the Reagan administration. Reagan, preferring a *laissez-faire* ocean where United States' companies were free to exploit ocean resources, cast a negative vote and the new ocean law was created in a crippled form without United States support. Thus cooperative management of the oceans awaits an American administration supportive of the objective. Still, considerable groundwork toward the development of ocean law and ocean administration has been achieved in spite of recent United States influence. A new political entity larger than any one country would permit integrated ocean planning at a world level. It would also reduce poor nation dependency on rich nations.

Educational Models

1. Grenville Clark and Louis B. Sohn published their first edition of *World Peace Through World Law* in 1958. It is possibly the most carefully developed transition plan for moving the world out of the war system. It proposes a revised United Nations Charter that transforms

the United Nations into a limited world government with authority to adjudicate and enforce peacekeeping between nations. The original publication is available in a concise summary that is useful for schools and public discussion.[3]

This proposal integrates disarmament, peacekeeping, world law, economic development, and human rights into a transition plan sensitive to the political considerations in moving from one kind of world system to another. The proposal is an excellent starting point for what would inevitably be a modified plan for actual United Nations Charter revision.

2. The Institute for World Order began in 1961 under the name World Law Fund. Saul Mendlovitz and Richard Falk undertook the first major collation and synthesis of academic materials bearing on war prevention, published in a series of volumes in the later 1960s. These publications, plus new world order theory, challenged the academic community to shift to problem-solving instead of conventional, passive, descriptive scholarship based on acceptance of the international system.

Betty Reardon worked with teachers to develop materials to introduce the new "world order studies" in the schools. By 1975, the National Council for the Social Studies had recognized world order education as a legitimate part of a social studies curriculum. By then the objectives included the problems of war, poverty, human rights, and ecological destruction, and many institutions of higher education had begun offering degrees or programs in peace studies, often making use of these world order materials.

Another project of the Institute for World Order, planned and directed by Saul Mendlovitz, had regional teams through the world working on models that would help realize a world-without-war system with values that would make sense within the cultural context of each region. One purpose of these "world order models" was to avoid a dominating Western perspective which might limit the willingness of non-Western nations to cooperate. This has been the most ambitious political design project yet undertaken. It is now completed and is being used in higher education throughout the world to further understanding of ways of shifting from the war system.

3. In 1969 the author of this book introduced into the teacher education program at the University of Hawaii a class called *Education for a World Without War* as well as a program called *War/Peace Program for Teachers*, which later became a part of graduate teacher education.

4. For the last ten years Arthur Pearl, a professor of education at the University of California at Santa Cruz, has been helping teachers develop an advanced approach to citizenship education which takes account of the need for a more liveable environment, full employment opportunity, transformation of the war system, and equal opportunity for minorities. Students have had to think through the very questions that now face political parties—how to contribute to the changes needed for survival, justice, and a high quality of life.

5. The University of California in 1983 was developing a statewide project for the various California campuses, based on research directed toward eliminating thermonuclear war. The project will be called the *Institute on Global Conflict and Cooperation* and will be coordinated through the San Diego, University of California campus.

6. Prior to the 1978 election of delegates to Hawaii's State Constitution Convention, two political science professors at the University of Hawaii (Ted Becker and Richard Kosaki) offered a political science class called Simulated Constitutional Convention. Students identified and researched issues, proposed constitutional amendments, and voted for those that were most persuasive. When the actual state election for delegates was held, a number of these students ran and some were elected. The proposals developed in class were influential in considerations that were used in constructing a new constitution, and students participated in hearings when the new constitution was being developed. The class was a model for citizenship and social change.

7. Since the early 1970s the Club of Rome has sponsored important studies which can aid integrated planning. One result was the well-known book *Limits to Growth* by Dennis and Donela Meadows, which compared various alternative futures based on conflict between limited resources and exponentially expanding population and production. The principles of a steady-state model are now well known. A number of the conflicts projected in this study have since been confirmed. A series of other studies by the Club of Rome have subsequently been published, providing helpful ways to approach integrated long-range international planning.[4]

Environmental Planning

The United Nations has sponsored two developments of considerable value to global planning. The first was the Universal Declaration of Human Rights, adopted by the General Assembly in 1948, which gave more precise expression to the kinds of rights that could gain universal support and serve as a foundation for future world law. The second was the creation of the United Nations Environmental Program, with its research center in Nairobi, Kenya. This program added environmental objectives to the previous UN framework of peacekeeping and social objectives. By giving special attention to the preindustrial countries, it encouraged the objective of combining development and sound environmental planning. Meanwhile, the research information base provided by UNEP is of vital importance to future integrated world planning.

Energy

Both energy conservation and improved air quality were encouraged by federal requirements on automobiles sold in the United States from the mid-1970s on. By providing year-by-year increases in required air quality and automobile gasoline mileage, the federal government used industry regulation to serve environmental quality and gasoline conservation.

Though the automobile companies were highly resistant to such regulations, they developed cleaner, more fuel-efficient automobiles that helped them compete with the small engine compacts being produced in Japan and Europe. But the government imposed "fleet" requirements for automobile fuel mileage standards that permitted manufacturers to meet the requirements of the law if their automobiles met a fleet average. This has meant that by manufacturing some high mpg automobiles manufacturers could continue to produce and sell the same old gas guzzlers. But even fleet average requirements helped the automobile industry serve the public interest.

Marginal Utility and the Quality of Life

Our grandparents knew that high consumption and high waste were not necessary for a good life. Their conserving habits were altered by a generation that grew up in the high-growth period following World War II. But many people have begun to mature beyond this period of economic adolescence and "doing more with less" has become an increasingly popular concept for those who have learned to distinguish quality of life from quantity of consumption.

A book called *The Conserver Society: A Workable Alternative for the Future*[5] represents this philosophy as not only one of acceptance of limits but also one of recognizing the *advantages* of accepting limits. The *Aquarian Conspiracy*[6] also advocates ways in which life can be good without high economic consumption.

A simple principle, based on marginal utility, can liberate people from constantly striving for more wealth and more consumption. The distance between not having a house and having one is very great. The distance between having a large high-tech house and a modest house is much smaller. Equally, assuming current mass transit to be inadequate, the distance between having no car and having a used Toyota is very great but the distance between having the Toyota and having a Mercedes is much smaller.

By applying the same principle to all the other things an economy can offer, we find that once we achieve a basic adequate level of consumption and the income of the middle class, the payoff for increased effort, increased expenditure, and increased consumption becomes increasingly trivial. People who have learned this lesson move from wealth and income goals to time-off goals, from high-paying, stressful, boring, or disgusting jobs to lower paying jobs with higher satisfaction. The following chart illustrates how increased costs produce marginal satisfactions. People who ignore this principle are often locked into obsessive status games and the morass of perpetual debt.

FIGURE 5.1 Diminishing Advantages

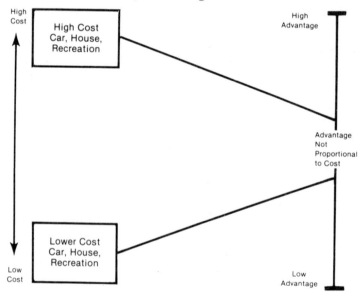

If the high-cost car, house, and recreation require a job that reduces personal integrity, job satisfaction, and time flexibility, the increase in income may well result in a net loss in quality of life.

Personal and public planning should focus on total quality of life instead of quantity of income. Many Americans are glutted with things which own them as much as they own the things. Ownership is always reciprocal, and a sustainable future based on renewable energy and low pollution fits nicely with a society that consumes less.

NATIONAL GOALS AND PRIORITIES

Long-range goals based on a set of value priorities are necessary for transition planning. Transition is *from* one era *to* another, and if there is to be a rationale for the improvement of the human condition the elements of a planned future must include (1) where we are, (2) what values we wish to maximize, (3) the specific goals that would include those values, and (4) transition steps.

For example, the following three values can be used:

Survival

Social justice

Quality of life

Though we should pursue all three values simultaneously through planning and public policy, our first priority should be *survival*, for all other goals depend on the continuity of human life. The most overriding threat to the continuity of human life at this period of human history is thermonuclear war. But war, poverty, and ecological destruction are all killers.

Lack of food kills those who live in poverty; the wrong food kills those who live in affluence. Food is the current number one killer in affluent countries, accounting for most of the heart failures and strokes, for diabetes, and for about half the cancer. Death from polluted water is a major killer in poor countries, but death from polluted air, water, and direct chemical contamination kills many Americans. Radioactivity could become a serious killer.

The following outline offers a model of goals, priorities, and transition steps that would permit us to get from here to there.

A Basic Transition Model

Value Affirmed:	From:	Transition Steps:	To:
S U R V I V A L	A War System	Arms control Disarmament World law Conflict mediation Standing police force	A Global Peacekeeping System
S U R V I V A L	A Poverty System	World economic planning Representative politics Economic manage-ment: human rights tools	Economic justice
S U R V I V A L	An Ecocide System	Giving ecosystem priority over economics Stability— sustainable energy (solar) Recycling	Sustainable economics within carrying capacity of life-support system
S U R V I V A L	Death from Diet 1. Too little in poor countries	More equitable distribution of food and land ownership in poor countries	Health from food
	2. Too much in rich countries	Economic and educational change from meat/dairy food to starch-centered diet Shift toward preventive medicine	Health from food
S U R V I V A L	Death from Environ-ment: Air, Water	Stronger enforce-ment of air/water standards in open areas and workplace Transportation/ work replanning	Health from environment

Value Affirmed:	From:	Transition Steps:	To:
S O C I A L	Economic Maldistribution:	Explicit distribution-ratio goals to guide tax revision and subsidy and ownership rights	Distribution equity
J U S T I C E	Too Few Human Rights in United States No Human Rights in parts of the world	Identify basic needs: food, education, medical, work, income floor	More positive rights in United States Global rights tied to world law
Q U A L I T Y O F L I F E	Environmental ugliness Crowding and congestion Noise High Crime	Urban design, natural preservation Land use, population dispersal planning Live near work— better mass transit Strict engine and construction noise requirements Employment opportunity Speedy trials and predictable penalties	Environmental beauty Density planning Quiet Safety on streets and in home

Value Affirmed:	From:	Transition Steps:	To:
Q		Community organization	
U			
A			
L	Pollution	Strong air, water control	Clean environment
I			
T		Criminal penalties	
Y			
O	Media Chaos with Commercial Domination	Reduced commercial time	Higher educational and cultural quality
F		Loss of advertising as business expense	
L			
I		Low-cost broadcaster access	
F			
E		More public radio/ TV	
Q			
U	Work/Leisure Imbalance	Flexible work times	More interesting work—more free time
A		Job sharing	
L		Shorter work week	
I			
T	Job Insecurity	Job creation in private sector and public service employment for job guarantee and retraining	The right to a job
Y			
O			
F			
L	Community disintegration	More cooperatives	Community integration
I		More groups involved in politics	
F		More democratic participation in government and economics	
E			

Fairness should include fairness between generations. Current generational exploitation leaves the young, the unborn, and the unconceived with pollution, debt, and diminished resources. Fairness also requires an economy built on principles of sustainability with protection for the environmental health of people, plants, and animals.

But the quality of life value has the most subjective and cultural considerations. Some standards can be universal such as economic security, preserving personal dignity, political and economic participation, lack of noise, freedom of expression, preservation of natural beauty, access to knowledge and information. But the design of cities, the degree of autonomy, and population density have strong elements of cultural and personal preference. So quality of life goals require the most decentralized participation and local application.

DESIGNING DISTRIBUTION

In the United States the top 0.5 percent of the population controls over 25 percent of the nation's privately held wealth and yearly income. Before resource and energy limitations led us into a period of slow growth, this maldistribution was ignored in public policy. A growth economy was designed to move everyone up, even though some went up faster than others. From here on, however, the economy will never have the same high growth rate, so those who get big pieces of this limited pie leave others with small pieces, or no pie at all.

If we are to remedy this situation, we must induce public policy to face the ethics of economic distribution and we must reduce the corruption of public planning that results from the way wealth can influence politics. The "one person one vote" principle is now highly distorted by the power of money, and money is very unequally distributed. Supply usually exceeds purchasing power because many people do not get adequate income from their labor, while others get too much.

It is important to clarify the three methods of economic distribution: (1) The Conservative Model—Accept the results of the market; (2) The Liberal Model—Use the market and redress negative effects with government programs and safety nets; and (3) The Social Ethics Model—Designate wealth-income ratios as public policy goals and use planning to move towards these goals. This third alternative would guide the planning of and the drafting of laws designating minimum and maximum wealth, appropriate taxes, subsidy, controls, regulations, and employment. There has never been an explicit ethical goal in American public policy aimed at achieving a reduction in relative poverty. Conservatives have advocated letting ratios result from market forces, liberals have advocated moderating market forces with minor ratio reductions coming from the political power of those injured by the market forces. Only this third proposal is based on using explicit social ethics for *planning* a fairer distribution of opportunities and outcomes. This would be an ethical step forward as a humane and civilized country faced up to economic justice and arranged the rules of the economic/political game to achieve those outcomes. It would require deflation of the myth that people *deserve* what they *get* in the American economy.

The ratio that would be targeted might not be anywhere near total equality of distribution, nor would it need to be in order to confront basic questions of economic justice. Some people would prefer to work harder to earn more, to sacrifice longer in preparing skills through education, and people at different age levels may need more income. But by stipulating explicit fairness standards, as for instance a macrodistribution ratio by the end of the century that Sweden achieved during the 1970s—1 to 7 between the top and bottom 10 percent—we would provide continuity and direction in public policy and planning and a graduated and predictable movement toward greater economic justice.

Thurow makes an interesting suggestion for a fair distribution ratio: use the distribution of fully employed white males. The income spread for this group is only one fifth as large between the top and bottom 20 percent as for the rest of the population consisting of women and of minorities.[7] White males do not have the history of discrimination of women and minorities and they are usually the hiring in-group. Addressing the question of whether incentive would be lost if inequality were reduced in the total working population, Thurow states:

> The West Germans work hard with 36% less inequality (between the top and bottom 10%) than we, and the Japanese work even harder with 50% less inequality. If income differentials encourage individual initiative, we should be full of initiative, since among industrialized countries only the French surpass us in terms of inequality.[8]

The principle of economic fairness that has been dominant in the American past is to have equal opportunity to compete. An educationally and economically "open" and "free" society has been a prerequisite to such equality.

Unequal opportunities have always produced unequal outcomes. Racial and religious discrimination have hindered access to jobs and income, while at the other end of the scale the private school system, so well developed in the New England states, has been a way of providing unequal opportunity for the children of the wealthy. Elite preparatory schools and exclusive and expensive colleges and universities have paralleled the British system of retaining upper class social control through education.

The twentieth century has produced increasingly equal access to schools and increasingly open access to jobs and income. But even now the disadvantages to minorities and women have not been overcome. Low costs in community colleges and in state higher education were major instruments for open access to the more coveted forms of employment until the depression of the 1980s converted educational institutions into conveyor belts directed mainly toward industrial and military related employment—engineering, physics, chemistry, business, ROTC.

Job access during the high growth of the 1960s and 1970s opened many opportunities to minorities, but slow growth and depression economics have put the lid on much access. This is an historically appropriate time to change rules of economic inequality that were tolerated under previous high growth. Current maldistribution arises especially from the following rules and procedures:

Interest deductions on personal housing, favoring the wealthy (and encouraging wasteful, large houses).

Taxing of unearned income such as capital gains at a lower level than income. Distributive fairness would certainly suggest the reverse.

Use of monopolistic control of prices in law and medicine.

Land upzoning, usually producing unearned private wealth when value added is not recaptured for public use.

Rapid investment depreciations, which provide tax advantages for the wealthy.

Price supports, favoring producers instead of consumers.

Corporate administering of prices.

Corporate administering of executive salaries, including their own.

Low cost access to minerals on public land.

Depletion allowances for minerals.

Military materials expenditure without competitive bids.

High interest rates which shift income from low-income borrowers to high-income lenders.

Economic maldistribution is not accidental, and its cure will not be accidental either. It will require deliberate action to narrow the range of wealth and income in the United States. Ironically, even while the United States is involved in a severe depression, the number of millionaires and billionaires is increasing at a record rate. The rules and procedures cited above are achieving their reverse Robin Hood objectives. They take from the poor and middle class and give to the rich and the Pentagon.

TWENTY-FIRST CENTURY HEALTH

Twentieth-century health planning greatly extended nineteenth century achievements in public health through sanitation in foods, water, sewage and in medical control of bacterial infections. Smallpox, once a scourge, has been eradicated. Tuberculosis, caused by poverty and bacteria, has been greatly reduced by better living standards and medical treatments. Infant mortality, especially in the developed nations, has dropped so considerably that longevity has changed drastically. However, although developed nations congratulate themselves on longer life spans, the statistics are based mainly on the survival rate of the newborn. Developed nations have cut back some forms of illness but have significantly added to others. They currently are a poor model for twenty-first century health.

World health problems in poor countries are caused mainly by too little food and by environmental contamination. In rich countries sickness and premature death can be laid in large part to the wrong food, too much food, environmental chemical contamination, and smoking. Environmental radiation may become significant in the future.

Natural longevity is now estimated to be in the nineties, but most Americans die at least twenty years too soon, mainly because of heart failure, stroke, cancer, and diabetes. These are caused mainly by the wrong kind of food. The high-fat diet accounts for about 40 percent of the cancer in men and 60 percent in women. Breast cancer (fat-caused) accounts for the 20 percent difference.[9]

Transition from a pathological diet has begun for many people, and with increased exercise levels, the incidence of heart problems has experienced a slight reduction for the first time this century.

In spite of some remarkable medical advances in the treatment of bacterial disease and in prosthetic replacements, medicine has very little effect on mortality. Figures on disease and death *caused* by medicine, especially in hospitals, largely offset the life-saving contributions. Because such a large portion of medical attention is given to diagnosis and treatment rather than prevention, public attention has been deflected from doing things that could have significant effects on health and longevity. These consist of changing eating habits, stopping smoking, and changing chemical environments usually connected with industry. The medical profession has increasingly supported the elimination of smoking, but doctors have been so poorly trained in nutrition that they have largely ignored it or have given poor advice. They are timid about industry-caused pathologies because they are usually politically allied with the corporate establishment. When the collusion of being part of a medical/pharmaceutical complex is added, the structural conflicts of interest become additional barriers. As a result medicine and health are different, and any increase in public health must begin with an understanding of the large *environmental* component of health and of how politics and education can be used to increase health and longevity.

What we do not need to do is to institute a national *medical* plan which we proceed to call a *health* plan. We do need a national health policy based on the best research related to health. Medical care should be included, but health and the *prevention* of sickness should be the main focus.

The medically oriented approach to "health," along with the Pentagon's approach to national security, are two factors leading toward national economic bankruptcy, for costs in both areas move upward exponentially, far in excess of the increase in real GNP. Continuation of such costs moves toward a time when expenses could equal total GNP. An effective policy which helped increase health could add significantly to both longevity and quality of life, and could shift economic resources into other areas of social need.

Integrated global health planning can begin with recognition that most poor people lack food and most rich people have too much food. Americans often believe they provide a breadbasket for food to poor countries. In fact, the United States *imports* more animal protein *from* poor countries than it exports. Because of market distribution the poor feed the rich the foods least needed by the rich and most needed by the poor. Peru's anchovies are used for animal feed in the rich countries in an amount that would raise the protein level of the entire South American continent to the southern European level.[10]

Poor countries import somewhat more grain from the United States than they export but most exported American grain goes to the wealthy nations to feed their animals. The consumed animal products then produce increases in heart attack, cancer, and diabetes in the general population.

Rich countries concentrate on producing the wrong *kind* of food, meats and dairy products, high in cholesterol and low in fiber. These are central to the pathology of diet in rich countries. The animals used for such food are usually the ones who have eaten the good food such as grains which in fact the people should be eating. When grains are fed to poultry and cattle, only a small part of the nutrition in the grain is finally available as food. The Soviets are locked into the same dietary habits; they import grains, often from the United States, to feed the animals they eat. This energy loss—resulting from eating the animal that eats the food—ranges from about a 70 percent loss with poultry to a 90 percent loss with beef. Range-fed animals are more efficient in capturing energy for they consume vegetation not used by people, though the ecological impacts on the land are often not worth the return.

There is a double payoff when proper nutrition planning occurs. People in rich countries can have a more healthy diet with significantly less heart failure, stroke, cancer, and diabetes, and more food would be available for the poor.

Dependency of poor nations on rich nations for basic food would, however, be very bad planning. Poor nations might be held as political hostages when their lifeline depends on rich nations. International conflicts which cut off transportation can produce mass starvation. Food shortages caused by disease and weather in the rich nations can produce export reductions and severe conflicts.

In addition, fresh food has the most nutrition. Storage and transportation contributes to contamination by insects and rodents. When grains are stored in tropical countries, the mold can produce aflatoxin, which causes liver cancer (a scourge in Africa). Even more, population increases, which eventually govern survival and quality of life, need to be confronted with realistic and perceived limits. Local food carrying capacities can be one indication of such a limit. And, in a world in which energy limits are also being approached, local food growing can save much transportation energy.

Health planning becomes a clear example of the need for integrated planning in which a number of things are done at the same time. When fruit is sent to the United States from Central America while children in Central America are starving, the solution is not the aggregate increase in food production but in the politics of distribution. People rarely die because of lack of food in their country; they do die because the market system of distribution prevents the poor from being able to afford food. They also die because they have moved from rural areas in to cities, often as a result of the "green revolution," a capital intensive form of agriculture. Industrial countries also use large labor forces in cities to serve the development of concentrated industry. People living in more decentralized rural countries have better access to food supplies, but when people are processed as labor during industrialization, they become dependent on monetary income for survival. When they get low wages or none at all, they are likely to suffer malnutrition and disease. China, with its huge population, has been the most successful poor country in avoiding starvation because of the retention of decentralized farm villages and a commitment to distribution politics. India, on the other hand, has drawn people into the cities and left their fate to the market. There is plenty of food for the affluent in India but not for the poor.

Typically, Americans have presumed that food problems are solvable mainly through technology—new genetic strains and large scale farms using large machines, petroleum-based fertilizers and ecology damaging pesticides. The objective is to maximize production and minimize labor, therefore increasing profit. If the objective is good nutrition for people rather than only maximizing profit for farmers, the planning objectives of agriculture will be tied to public health. The current distribution system for food in the United States is largely a part of the health problem. School lunches are based more on farm excesses than the kind of diet (starch-centered with grains, fruit, and vegetables) on which good health is based. Restaurants are usually carnivores' dens, almost always basing the "entree" on meat.

The current fad in the United States is weight reduction, so people often lose weight through ways that threaten their health. People can be thin, unhealthy, and atherosclerotic. But if they eat properly, they will not be fat; they usually will be healthy and their circulatory system will not be clogged.

Being overweight is only a possible clue to being unhealthy, though one can be thin and unhealthy. If being overweight is caused by nonfat-based calories such as sugar or alcohol, the dangers of heart attack and cancer are not high. But if one is overweight and consumes fat at usual Western levels (three times as much as is needed) poor health and early death are likely.

With the amount of information now available about health, nearly as many people know about good diet as know about the dangers of smoking. Who should pay for the social costs of people who opt for voluntary illness? Should the costs of medical treatment for the smoker and for the person whose cholesterol level is high because of incorrect diet be paid by other members of society or by the person who is at fault? Are we not entering an age where we need to deal differently with those who choose illness than with those who choose health?

Those who smoke are not paying for the total costs of cigarettes which produce a high incidence of emphysema and lung cancer plus many other maladies. If a dollar-a-pack tax were put on cigarettes, it might be used to compensate for some of the Medicaid, Medicare, and private insurance costs now paid by the nonsmoker. It may even be advisable to do the same with meats and dairy products. People with cholesterol levels above the health range, 140 to 180 mg, could be expected to contribute to health insurance costs proportionally according to cholesterol levels to cover later costs of their voluntary illness.

Those who experience costs not of their own choosing or not avoidable by intelligent action deserve the social sharing of costs. *But the system of social compassion can be destroyed if irresponsible people and responsible people receive the same benefits.* The burden of costs becomes exponential, and there is a loss of the sense of fairness that must underly successful public policy.

Therefore, in integrated health planning the human right to modern medical care must be qualified as automobile insurance costs are on the basis of driving records. But to do this requires an ample educational program in order that knowledge of diet and smoking can be presumed on the part of the general public.

Transition to a healthful diet involves learning new menus so healthful foods are also tasty. It involves extrication from the current agricultural-industrial-medical-pharmaceutical complex. It involves shifting of costs and benefits in medical payments. It involves new programs of public education which will reveal to low-income groups that eating in a more healthful way costs about 60 percent of the cost of the usual American diet. It involves the elimination of myths about children needing milk (high in cholesterol, devoid of fiber). Children in

China do not drink milk after weaning from the mother. The calcium myth is very important to the dairy industry, but foods without animal fat supply all the calcium needed. The new endurance athletes use starch—potatoes, rice, spaghetti—as a superior energy base rather than meat.

Transformation to a more healthy society will require that exercise and recreation, better food, and less pollution from smoking, transportation, and industrial sources be part of the planning. Tension reduction, through better economic security and fairer economic and political rules, is also related to health. Agriculture would focus on health instead of only profit. Farming would change from a depleter of topsoil and would become more land intensive, organic, and topsoil-regenerating, with less use of chemical fertilizer and pesticides. More nutritional, naturally adaptable crops would be produced. Elimination of feed-lot food production would cut down on pollutants in rivers, and if land were less pressed to produce for profit (less production being required if we eat lower on the food chains) there could be abundance of food and greater soil conservation. Starvation is unnecessary anywhere in the world at current population levels. Excess farm production should be transferred to energy production—alcohol and bio-gas. The amount of land used to produce energy would depend on food needs, which would be the first priority. And these earth-sustaining, energy-producing uses of farmland would be more labor intensive, producing more jobs.

JOBS AND TRANSITION

An integrated plan involving transition from one era to another should focus on the elements that hold the present system intact. The key element is employment. *What we are employed to do is the main factor that defines the economic system and determines the direction in which we are going.* People hold tightly to any activity that provides them with their livelihood. Almost any political rationalization will develop to try to justify the need for the continuation of that job. Once a military-industrial complex becomes a major part of an economy, as it has in the United States, it is very difficult to dismantle it, for people who profit by it will find "reasons" for its continuation. They will even become spokesmen for specific weapons systems. In times of unemployment such economic lock-in psychology will intensify.

Change strategy requires countering the threat of job loss with employment alternatives that open new opportunities. Only then can people assess the social value of basic change proposals. Transition goals can most easily be achieved if employment changes can involve economic advantages in the form of *job satisfaction* or a more *attractive place to live*. Without these guarantees there can be no real consideration of new national goals.

In the past new goals have developed only when (1) there has been so much unemployment that there were discontented people to force change, or (2) there has been so much economic growth that there were many job choices and little economic insecurity.

A third method, advocated in this book, is to plan the development of a survival-based peace economy with many new jobs which permit people to do socially useful work without loss of income. This requires social priorities, environmental constraints, and dismantling of the military-industrial economy.

Because military expenditure produces so few jobs relative to other forms of expenditure, it is very difficult to have full employment opportunity without de-militarization.[11] It is also clear that our first-priority goal, survival, also demands de-militarization in this nuclear era.

Since the depression of the 1930s, all Keynesian growth stimulation, promoted particularly by the Democratic party, has used expansion of the military-industrial complex as a major part of the stimulus to growth. Such military-based growth will produce an increase in monetary GNP (though not in jobs) even though much of that Gross National Product is a war product (truly a gross product). But liberals have either joined the arms race camp with the conservatives or have not been able to get a majority in Congress who would support full employment *through a civilian economy*. The myth of national security through a nuclear arms race, the myth of prosperity through military spending, and the ideological belief that employment should depend on the private sector have produced full employment paralysis. The Employment Act of 1946 never guided national employment policy for the above reasons. "Full" was a misnomer, requiring the President to present to Congress a job plan when unemployment rose to unacceptable levels.

The Reagan depression provides an opportunity to realize transition through employment opportunities directed toward survival goals, social values, ecological restraints, and common quality of life goals. Yet given the severity of the depression intensified by Reagan there are grave dangers throughout the world that polarization and violence will be so incorporated in change that fascism and autocratic communism will be the emerging forms of politics. For those who define alternatives so narrowly that we must choose only between corporate capitalism and state repression, the chances for reform may be hopeless. *Our best current opportunity is to take the strong political arms-freeze movement and the strong pro-employment movement and give them a central role in a politics that also takes account of a number of other objectives.* Otherwise, employment groups, for example, might settle for jobs, whatever jobs, no matter whether they are ecologically destructive, of low social priority, or part of the war economy.

Planning for recovery is currently so primitive that it consists largely of desperate attempts on the part of cities to bring in any form of industry, though "high tech" is preferred. Major economic and land use concessions are being made to businesses and industries, some of which are using a form of blackmail to get preferential, subsidized treatment from city and state governments. The same tough strategy is being used on labor to break up unionization and to lower wages. Some businesses are themselves in danger of going broke under the stress of depression, but many have moved not because they are going broke but only to increase profits. With the tax write-offs provided under the Reagan administration and the loans, zoning variance, tax advantages, and pollution advantages being offered, the American corporate system is able to hold many people in hostage with threats to leave, as many do, if the grass is greener in a low-wage, nonunion country.

But now that corporations are increasingly abandoning America, even though Americans have not abandoned the corporations, this is an optimum time to withdraw from excessive dependence upon them. It is time for corporations in the private sector to have to begin competing or cooperating with economic activity in the public sector, for a planned economy does not have to let itself be hostage to self-interest corporations that treat the public interest as secondary.

Detroit made enormous concessions in taking large sections of downtown, rezoning them, eliminating residences and small businesses, and giving land to General Motors at such a subsidized rate that GM was willing to build a plant there. Otherwise the company threatened a city of high unemployment with a partial exodus to build the plant away from Detroit where subsidies would be most attractive.

The Detroit government was locked into the idea that employment could come only from the private sector. There was no study to find out how the public sector could create socially valuable employment with the same amount of money that was being given to General Motors. There was no cost-benefit measurement of the housing that was bulldozed and the lives that were uprooted. The people of Detroit did not run Detroit. General Motors was king.

If the *federal* government would keep a high corporate tax on companies such as General Motors and transfer that money to states according to their population, the company would have little economic incentive to run away from Detroit to another part of the United States. And if General Motors wanted to leave the country, state and federal funds could be used to create the transportation system, infrastructure, and vehicles that are needed. Instead of getting subsidized, Chrysler could then bid in competition with public corporations to contribute to such transportation—mass and private.

An even more feasible area for public business is in service industries—transportation, public radio, public television, cable TV, and mail. European countries have always assumed that rail and inter-city transportation should be subsidized to make sure that the economy can rely on good transportation and that low-income people can have access to basic transportation. Low cost opera has been publicly sponsored in Italy, and England has sytems of medicine and television with public subsidy and management that are models for quality and accessibility. The Canadian government operates its own airline which competes with a private air-line.

Any country that wants to make a substantial investment in becoming a "learning" society can open enormous opportunities for the employment of teachers in schools and through media. In the United States there are many unemployed or partially employed musicians and artists who are unable to survive as musicians and artists, though many are exceedingly competent. They would be aiding people of all ages in becoming musicians and artists if they were employed to do so. Recreational opportunities have only begun as ways to provide physical education, social education, and outdoor environmental education.

We need to view unemployment not as a matter of too many people but as a matter of too few jobs. There is no teacher surplus; there is a teaching job shortage. Unemployment in the United States does not result from the satiation of public needs but from economic mismanagement. Goods and services are not distributed well. Training and education required for economic change are either mismanaged or nonexistent.

Part of the problem has been lack of economic priorities so that a portion of the society is glutted with goods and services while other portions lack housing, transportation, food, medicine, clean air, clean water, quiet safe cities, nursing homes, good education, and an opportunity to make an economic contribution. If human needs are first priority goals, we need to recognize that relying on the rules of "market" production and distribution will usually exacerbate the maldistribution rather than solve it. Too little will trickle down, yet the disciplining of labor resulting from unemployment will be considered a valuable economic asset by many people with high wealth and income.

There is a contradiction in this view that comes back to haunt the rich, for even though there are higher profits in some corporations when labor costs are kept down, primitive labor practices often result in low productivity. And wage earners who lack the money to buy the goods and services do not have demand capacity to absorb production. When demand drops, profits drop, and depression results. Reagan flunked on this aspect of economics, for his "supply side" economics was based on increasing production in a country that did not have the demand-income to purchase what was being produced. He thought supply would produce demand, ignoring elementary economics that recognizes that in a market system demand produces supply.

Public Choice of the Future

Current American democracy is based on paternalism. Governors, presidents, and legislators are chosen as individuals who will, their supporters hope, do some worthwhile things for their constituency. We choose them because they seem the most honest and hardworking, and have values and ideology closer to our own than do the other candidates. We presume that the political power we give them will permit this governor, or this president, or this legislator to create a better future for us. But we, as citizens, never choose that future directly, because that is not the way the game has been designed. It is a muddling-through game in which there is no plan for the future of a state or the nation, no real alternative features we can debate and assess. The only direct choice of policy is through state initiatives, where propositions (California Proposition 13 is the most well known) are put to a vote. But this is different from choosing an integrated long-range plan.

What we should be doing is electing *the future* through a general plan for our state and our nation. Various groups could put together such plans, and drawing upon people with expertise, work out major alternatives that are feasible and sustainable. Debate on these substantive alternatives would precede an election, and if a majority was not obtained, there could be a runoff between the two top models. Such a plan might have a ten-year period subject to limited mid-course correction. *Governors, legislators, and presidents would know what their duty was under this kind of democracy: it would be to implement and create the future chosen by the public.* If they proved to be incompetent administrators, they would be fired. Legislation that came in conflict with the general plan would be unacceptable. The time for special interest groups to shape the future would be during the development of the general plan.

If Hawaii has been able to create a new constitution for itself every ten years, this proposal is no less feasible. Amendments to state constitutions and the federal constitution may be needed to create planning-government of the kind proposed. It may look difficult, but it is possible and imperative.

Law in the Twenty-first Century

The most significant changes needed in law are national constitutions which require integrated democratic planning and world law that holds people to international legal standards similar to law within a nation.

We must rewrite constitutions to include substantive law guaranteeing a right to employment, an ecologically sustainable economy, a clean and healthful environment, and rights of future generations. Other basic human needs should be similarly guaranteed to anyone willing to be a peaceful, law-abiding member of society who is also willing to contribute labor. Many forms of environmental destruction now considered minor offenses will need to be criminal offenses, and scarce nonrenewable resources that impact on the larger public will need to be put under public ownership or control.

Unless these substantive changes are put into the Constitution, the basic law of the land, they will be subject to constant legislative change based on special interest pressures. No long-range planning can be undertaken under such an obsolete system.

We will need simultaneous development of world law. Clearly there will be complicated issues to deal with, many of which will not be adequately handled by representatives of nation states, but such basic issues as the jurisdiction of the World Court over international disputes, violations of disarmament, and classification of any killing of a citizen of one country by a citizen of another as murder might be the core of the earliest world law.

In order to facilitate the creation of world law, an implementing body similar to the UN General Assembly must have representatives both from nation states and the public at large. This limited world government should possess authority over nations in dispute settlement and a police force that can stop international violence.

Ocean law and the creation of an ocean regime composed both of national representatives and the public at large would be epochal steps in political and legal institution building. The ecological management of the ocean's resources, especially for the use of the poor nations, has special possibilities as has the end of the tradition of freedom of the seas, a tradition which has often meant freedom for the most powerful navies and which is now being used by the most powerful nations and corporations to justify exploiting ocean resources—minerals, petroleum, whales, and fish—for their own self-interest. Ocean law which deals with ocean resources as common global heritage should end the movement to treat the ocean as a garbage dump for chemicals and radioactive waste.

A NEW POLITICS

The new politics we need can come only with new public expectations followed by effective political action. The following list is a set of minimum goals and principles, offered as a way to test political candidates and platforms. Based on the assumption that politics should further survival, social justice, and a high quality of life, a party's or candidate's specific policies should support:

- Integrated planning of the economy and environmental resources.
- Rights to employment with government responsibility to provide employment.
- A sustainable economy that does not deplete or degrade resources.
- A federal plan for transition to a renewable energy base.
- World law and UN peacekeeping instead of national military power as the basis for war prevention.
- Transition plans for economic conversion from a war economy.
- Direct public selection of the best of the alternative state and federal integrated plans.

- Executive and legislative responsibility to implement the integrated plans.
- National and global human rights, including rights to a clean and healthful environment and rights of future generations.
- National priorities based on basic human needs.
- Both national and direct public representation in the UN.
- Designation of a national income and wealth distribution ratio as a basis for tax reform.

The current willingness to tolerate high unemployment rates tells much about the current dilemma of American politics. It reveals the confusion of Americans about connections between politics and economics. An informed public would sweep candidates out of power if they tolerated large-scale unemployment. The pain and suffering of millions of Americans who are unemployed can occur only in a modern nation that does not know what to expect from government.

Once we believe the "best government is the least government," there is no obligation for government to provide basic conditions of economic security and human decency and to help promote the higher qualities in people rather than the lower ones. The unemployed and the poor receive the public contempt which is more appropriate for those who permit poverty and unemployment to continue unchecked.

At the root of our common problems are beliefs about our obligations and our power. If we have a sense of obligation toward each other we have gone part of the distance toward a better society. A society of people with a sense of obligation toward only themselves will lack the qualities needed to permit people to achieve even their own self-interest, for the social cost of people preying on each other rather than cooperating is enormous.

However, a growing minority of people are engaged in the new history-creating process. They achieve self-respect and a sense of significance much more rewarding than only economic payment. They help create the future through their own choices; they both affirm life and understand the importance of political power. They aid in creating open dialogue to widen public participation in ideas and issues, but they connect thought and action and focus on the central questions of political action. They recognize that goals, even long-range ones, are necessary to permit one to know what is most worth doing *now*, for what we do or fail to do now governs the kind of future we will have.

The new politics is therefore tied not only to achievement but to becoming a better person. The process is self-rewarding. If the human race is to respond successfully to the crises of our age, a sense of citizenship is required which ancients such as Plato and Aristotle understood. But the new meaning of politics and community building goes beyond the Greeks and makes the definitions of progress implicit in capitalism, Marxism, and the Reformation obsolete. It avoids both determinism and mysticism and evaluates existing institutions in relation to human rights, global environment, and the application of technology to humane uses.

Worldwide protests against nuclear war and the arms race indicate how millions have become politicized by the pathological obsolescence of an institution that in the name of defense moves toward holocaust.

Politics that tries to gain its credibility by being incredible can lead some to the dangerous belief that all politics is inherently absurd. The future will be built by those who demand a better politics. Millions have been able to see through a secretary of the interior who sells out public resources in the name of preserving our public heritage. Secretaries of state who cry freedom but support right-wing dictators are no longer acceptable to educated modern citizenry. New candidates, parties, and platforms can expect more and more rigorous scrutiny than in the past, aided by the rapidly expanding set of organizations and networks that permit everyone to support lobbyists. Though this has led to a fragmentation of political interest groups, those enlisted in the common causes of war prevention and the demand for a livable environment are now ready to produce political consensus that cannot be ignored.

Ethics and politics are being connected. Ecumenical religious groups work against despotic governments and for humane politics. Catholic bishops have publicly denounced the arms race and the specific arms policies of the Reagan administration. The Vatican has actively entered the struggle against nuclear war. Intervention in Central America to continue the old gunboat diplomacy which tried to make the world safe for American capitalism is losing public support.

The National Education Association and the National Council for Social Studies have prepared and authorized studies of war and peace and world order in the public schools. There are about 30 undergraduate institutions of higher education in the United States offering an academic major or a certificate in peace studies. An increasingly larger number of professors of political science have shifted from international studies to world order studies.[12]

We must give new meaning to the term "basic education" so that it includes not merely computational and literary skills but also political understanding incorporated into citizenship education. In particular, students should have opportunities to learn about planning, a study now reserved for professional planners in graduate school. Planning, in fact, should be the instrument for synthesizing fields of knowledge, including ethics, so that alternatives in public policy are understood. Students should be attending and participating in public meetings involving planning decisions. Schools would then become our centers of political education, vital and relevant to the real world.

Clubs, businesses, unions, the press, radio, TV, environmental organizations, churches, and other groups can increasingly be educational and political agencies that help people create the future. They can stand out in front of government and illuminate direction. They can also represent the sources of votes and electoral power to make sure they are heard.

The struggle to change habits and institutions that have treated dominance and exploitation as rights will not be easy. Yet the nuclear freeze movement reveals how public movements can gain rapid power, even though no basic political change has as yet occurred. Now the movement's leaders must frame long-range goals so that we are not seeking merely disarmament but are starting along the road to security in the nuclear age.

The central political challenge before us today is to create law that will establish both justice and peace. To do this we must learn to use political power to control our institutions not only that we may have a better life but that we may continue to have life at all.

NOTES

1. Harrison Brown, "Scenario for an American Renaissance," *Saturday Review* (Dec. 25, 1971).

2. *Oregon Lands* (Sept. 1978), Vol. 1, No. 5. Also, *Statewide Planning Goals and Guidelines*, Oregon Dept. of Land Conservation and Development, Salem, Oregon.

3. Grenville Clark and Louis B. Sohn, *World Peace Through World Law* (Cambridge, MA: Harvard University Press, 1958).

4. Mihajlo Mesarovic and Eduard Pestel, *Mankind at the Turning Point* (New York: E. P. Dutton, 1974). Jan Tinbergen, et al., *RIO: Reshaping the International Order*.

5. Kimon Valaskais, et al., *The Conserver Society* (New York: Harper, 1979).

6. Marilyn Ferguson, *The Aquarian Conspiracy* (New York: Houghton Mifflin, 1980).

7. Lester C. Thurow, *The Zero-Sum Society* (New York: Basic Books, 1980), p. 202.

8. Ibid., pp. 7–8.

9. Report by the National Academy of Sciences, *Diet, Nutrition, and Cancer* (Washington, DC: National Academy Press, 1982). Carmel Reingold, *The Lifelong Anti-Cancer Diet* (New York: Signet, 1982).

10. George Borgstrom, *Too Many: A Study of Earth's Biological Limitations* (New York: MacMillan, 1969), p. 237. George Kent, "Food Trade: The Poor Feed the Rich," *Food and Nutrition Bulletin* (Oct. 19, 1982).

11. See Chapter 4 for employment figures.

12. William H. Boyer, "World Order Studies: What Is It?" (*Phi Delta Kappan*, April, 1975), pp. 524–27.

SELECTED READINGS

Barnet, Richard. 1981. *Real Security*. New York: Simon and Schuster.

Barney, Gerald O., Director. *The Global 2000 Report to the President: Entering the Twenty-first Century*. Washington, DC: Supt. of Documents.

Boyer, William H. 1972. *Education for Annihilation*. Honolulu: Hogarth-Hawaii. Available from the author.

Brown, Lester. *Redefining National Security*. Washington, DC: Worldwatch Institute No. 14, Oct. 1977. Also Lester Brown, *Resource Trends and Population Policy: A Time for Reassessment*. Washington, DC: Worldwatch Paper No. 29, May 1979.

Eckholm, Erik P. 1977. *The Picture of Health*. Washington, DC: Worldwatch Institute.

Epstein, William. 1976. *The Last Chance*. New York: The Free Press.

Hawken, Paul, et al. 1982. *Seven Tomorrows*. New York: Bantam.

Hayden, Tom. 1980. *The American Future*. Boston: South End Press.

Heller, Alfred, ed. 1971. *The California Tomorrow Plan*. Los Altos, CA: William Kaufman.

Johnson, Warren. 1978. *Muddling Toward Frugality*. New York: Random House.

Laszlo, Ervin. 1974. *A Strategy for the Future*. New York: George Braziller.

Leff, Herbert. 1978. *Experience, Environment, and Human Potentials*. New York: Oxford University Press.

Marsh, Leonard. 1973. *Education in Action: Proposals for a Social Planetarium*. Vancouver, BC: Versatile.

Marsh, Leonard. 1973. *Education in Action: Proposals for a Social Planetarium*. Vancouver, BC: Versatile.

Michael, Donald. 1968. *The Unprepared Society*. New York: Basic Books.

Sloan, Douglas, ed. *Education for Peace and Disarmament*. New York: Teacher's College Record, Vol. 84, No. 1, Fall 1982.

Appendix

Appendix:
A Transition Glossary

The terms presented here are organized under seven headings: *Biological Ecology*, *Human Population*, *Resources*, *Pollution*, *Values*, *Systems*, and *Planning*.

Biological Ecology: The interdependence of organisms, including people, with each other and with their physical environment.

Term	Concept
Biological control	The introduction of birds, animals, insects, or fish to control other organisms.
Community	The populations of all species that live in a particular area.
Cycles: Water, CO_2 carbon, nitrogen, phosphorus	Natural recycling systems of movement through an ecosystem, often through plants and animals activated by solar energy. The water cycle, for example, includes evaporation, rain, rivers, and ocean.
Decomposers	Organisms such as worms, bacteria, and fungi that eat dead organic material and convert it into nutrients.
Diversity	The complexity of a community.
Dominance	Control by a plant or animal of the largest portion of energy in a community.

Ecological niche	The unique function of a plant or animal in a biologial community; its place in the ecological system.
Endangered species	Plants, animals, fish, birds, or insect species that are being destroyed so rapidly that without better protection they may cease to exist.
Entropy	The loss of energy during energy transfer. All transfer in the food web involves entropy (the second law of thermodynamics).
Food webs	Interdependent feeding levels which involve transfer of energy and materials.
Nitrogen-fixing bacteria	Soil bacteria that convert inorganic nitrogen into usable plant nutrients.
Photosynthesis	The process by which green plants convert solar energy into chemical energy.
Plankton	Microscopic plants and animals found in lakes, rivers, and oceans; they are at the beginning of the food chain.
Symbiosis	An association of dissimilar organisms, producing mutual benefits.
Territoriality	A sense of possession of an area, which the possessor defends against intruders.
Watershed	A land area that catches rain and guides it above ground and underground into a common outlet.

Human Population: The numbers of people in any human community.

Term	Concept
Contraceptive	Mechanical, surgical, or chemical means of preventing pregnancy.
Doubling time	The time it takes for a population to double.
Exponential increase	Geometrical increase in population that accelerates the total numbers through doubling times: 1, 2, 4, 8, 16, 32, 64, etc.
Family planning	Having only the number of children per family that is desired by the husband and wife.

Population age distributions	The proportional numbers at various age levels. Countries differ in their distribution patterns.
Population mobility	Movements of people from one area to another, either in large numbers or continuous flows.
Zero population growth	Having only the number of births that replace deaths, so that the total population does not increase.

Resources: Natural and human materials and processes which people might use to serve human objectives. For example, resources can include minerals, food, and information.

Term	*Concept*
Energy	Capacity to do work. Work produces change but requires power. Energy makes plants grow, wind blow, and automobiles go. It permits us to think and move. Energy sources can come from stored fossil fuel, incoming solar energy, geothermal heat, tides, and fission and fusion nuclear sources.
Nonrenewable	Resources that are finite in amount, such as petroleum or minerals, and cannot be replaced if they are consumed or destroyed.
Nutrients	The chemical and biological elements that provide energy and growth to plants and animals.
Renewable	Resources that can be replaced when consumed or destroyed, such as wheat or fish.

Pollution: Contamination that reaches levels destructive to the maintenance of the quality of the life-support system.

Pollution can occur in air, water, land, and food and may be experienced through human senses.

Pollution can occur through *eutrophication*, which speeds up growth in water and fills in lakes and rivers with plants and sediments.

Pollution can occur through *toxification*, which either kills or injures the organism. For instance, automobile exhaust produces toxic pollution that makes "smog" which contributes to discomfort, illness, and death.

Values: Judgments of worth or desirability.

Term	Concept
Cooperation	People working together for the good of the group.
Democracy	Participation by members of a group in the formation of group rules and policies.
Equity	A fair distribution of the goods, services, and opportunities generated by an economic system.
Esthetic value	The quality of an experience, not instrumental to something else, but "good" in itself. Esthetic value combines understanding and feeling and can consist of the beauty of art, nature, or the style and quality of human behavior.
Ethical values	"The worth and dignity of the human person," applied to an assessment of human consequences of human actions. Ethical values can operate through direct interpersonal relations and also through indirect institutional action such as government, economics, and business.
Health	A state in which disease is absent, resistance to disease is high, and the body functions properly at a level of abundant energy.
Progress	A set of social changes seen as providing a better life for most of a society's members.
Quality of life	Environmental, social, and personal characteristics that contribute to the desirability of one's life.
Social ethics	The service of public values through the explicit social goals of political, economic, or institutional structures.

Systems: A set of interdependent parts where the whole is greater than the sum of its parts. There are *natural* physical and biological systems, *social* systems such as economic systems, and *technological* systems such as a highway system. Natural systems are created by nature; social and technical systems are invented by people.

Term	*Concept*
An ecocide system	A system in which political and economic rules determine that there will be progressive deterioration of the ecological life-support system.
A poverty system	A system in which political and economic rules determine that poverty will be the outcome.
A war system	A system in which anarchy and national sovereignty are the rules of international organization, and military violence instead of law is the instrument for the ultimate resolution of international conflict.
Closed system	A system with finite and fixed number of parts. Nonrenewable resources are part of a "closed system."
Open system	A system with expanding number of parts. Symbolic systems can be "open." Ideas and information can be increased without exhausting the supply.
Growth	Commonly used to mean the quantitative expansion of an economy which increases wages, profits, gross national product, and the amount of goods and services.
Interdependence	A system in which members rely on each other for their mutual benefit.
Life-support system	The air, soil, water, and heat on the surface of the earth that provide a basis for organisms and human life to survive through the development of ecological systems.
Malthusian	Referring to the theory of Thomas Malthus, an eighteenth-century economist,

who saw that if population expands geometrically while food expands at a slower rate, people would soon starve. The concept now refers to the dire consequences of permitting open expansion of population and consumption in a life-support system with limited resources.

No-growth system

A stagnant economic system that does not change significantly.

Steady-state system

A society and its economy in a state of ecological equilibrium which is able to keep the life-support system from deteriorating. A *dynamic* steady-state system reorganizes the economy to improve quality of life while also achieving ecological equilibrium.

Structural exploitation

The exploitation produced when a social system (poverty, ecocide, political, economic, or institutional) takes unfair advantage over some to provide advantages to others.

Structural murder

The destruction of human life by social systems such as the war system, the poverty system, and the ecocide system, which predetermine that unnecessary death will occur.

Structural violence

Violence produced by a social system (war, poverty, ecocide; political, economic, or institutional) because of the very nature of that system.

Supranational

Operating on a political level higher than national law or politics. World law or world government would be supranational.

Transnational

Extending beyond national identity. Religious and scientific groups can be transnational when they are not attached to national loyalties.

Tragedy of the commons

A parable environmentalists use to show how individual interests in exploiting natural resources contradict the survival needs of the community. If the common life-support system has finite resources, a procedure that permits individuals to use more than their fair share will cause destruction to the "commons." The commons can be land or any other limited resource.

Planning: Planning can be individual or social. It is a process used to decide on the best goals and the best means to achieve those goals. Social planning of cities and countries tries to reduce human dependence on random accidents and to permit common goals to be achieved and the future to be more predictable. City planning is now a common practice.

Term	*Concept*
Ad hoc	Piecemeal planning that responds with short-range solutions to separate problems.
Carrying capacity	The maximum capacity of an area to support a given population without destruction of the life-support system or the quality of life.
Cost/Benefit Analysis	Procedures for assessing whether there is more to be gained than to be lost by a plan. Cost/benefit analysis can include economic, social, and ecological considerations.
Environmental Impact Statement (E.I.S.)	An attempt to predict impacts on environment and may apply a cost/benefit analysis to a specific proposed project.
External costs	The cost paid by the larger society rather than by the manufacturer. For instance, there may be costs which a manufacturer pays to have garbage taken away, but the larger society may pay for the costs of the garbage dump, the pollution of ground water, and the loss of the resources in the

	garbage. The social cost can be in money, health, and quality of life.
Forecasting	Using scientific methods to anticipate the future; often involves projecting trends such as population increases to see where they are heading. Permits decisions on whether to change trends or adapt to them.
Futuristics	The study of the kinds of futures that are possible; it provides a basis for deciding which is the most desirable.
Integrative	Planning that takes account of a number of problems and goals simultaneously and aims toward both short- and long-range solutions.
Involuntary suicide	Killing oneself inadvertently because of lack of knowledge, such as of pollution or nutrition.
Irreversibility	Refers to an action or condition which prevents a second chance, such as when petroleum is burned or prime topsoil is lost to the point at which erosion or desert replaces a stable, productive ecosystem.
Lead time	The advance time it will take to develop a plan and put it into effect. Major changes in energy sources may take decades, e.g., shifting from one system (petroleum) to another (solar, etc.). Therefore, forecasting is necessary to anticipate the lead time.
Low-energy consumption technology	Machines and other kinds of technology which are designed to use minimum amounts of energy, such as a small car vs. a big car.
Overload	Exceeding carrying capacity.
Participatory planning	Democratic involvement by the community in the planning process.
Pesticides	Chemical technology for insect control. Specific pesticides kill a precise group of insects; broad-spectrum pesticides kill a great number of types of insects.

Political design	The establishment of a common future to be realized and of public policies and implementation to bring that future into being.
Priorities	Decisions that provide an order of importance for a number of planning objectives.
Trade-off	A decision (based on priorities) concerning what should be given up in order to achieve something else. Trade-offs are necessary when two objectives cannot both be achieved without some sacrifice of one or both objectives.
Voluntary suicide	Killing oneself directly or indirectly through actions such as smoking, driving fast, or eating injurious foods, even though one understands the consequences.
Zero-sum vs. non-zero sum	When scarce resources are divided among a limited number of people, the more some get, the less others get. If some win, others lose. Zero-sum applies to scarce resources and raises the question of equitable distribution. Zero-sum applies also to future generations: The petroleum used now is taken from future generations. In non-zero sum, abundant resources are created so no one has to lose what another gains.

Index

About the Author

William Boyer is Emeritus Professor of Education from the University of Hawaii, where he was professor in philosophy of education from 1961 to 1982. He taught at Stockton College, Milwaukee-Downer College, Chico State University, University of Montana, World Campus Afloat, and University of Oregon.

His courses have been within the fields of psychology, political science, and social foundations of education. He has developed programs and courses in war prevention, environmental education, comparative ideology, alternative futures, and public planning.

Dr. Boyer has published some 60 articles in professional journals and books, and his articles have also appeared in *Saturday Review*, *The Nation*, and *The Progressive*. His previous books were *Education for Annihilation* and *Alternative Futures: Designing Social Change*.

He now lives in Oregon, writing and lecturing primarily on education for preventing nuclear war.